FOOD FOREST REVOLUTION

WHY FOOD FORESTS EVERYWHERE COULD
CHANGE EVERYTHING

by Jennifer Taber Reelitz

Food Forest Revolution

Copyright 2024 by Jennifer Taber Reelitz

ISBN 979-8-218-42322-3 (paper)

ISBN 979-8-218-42323-0 (electronic)

Cover Photo by Olivia Sahnger

Cover Design by Melissa Moore

For information about special discounts for bulk purchases or to book an event please contact the author at jen@foodforestdiy.com.

FOOD FOREST DIY

www.foodforestdiy.com

Follow us on Instagram

@foodforestrevolution

@foodforestdiy

ACKNOWLEDGMENTS

There are many people to thank who inspired and encouraged me in this project.

First, I want to express my gratitude to one of my mentors, Heather Dorsey. Heather was the first gardener in my adult life to plant the seed of growing food in my mind and heart. She grew her own food forest, gifted me fruit trees every year on my birthday, and was an inspiration to me in a myriad of ways. I'm eternally grateful for her love and profound influence on my life. She is the kind of person I hope to become. After Heather lit the spark of passion for food forest, I started watching content on YouTube to learn all I could. The greatest influencer in my food forestry education was David the Good. In both his books and videos, he made food forest concepts simple. He's funny and relatable and made me believe that I could do it, too. I'd also like to thank Kimberly Webb Lague for inviting me to teach an edible landscaping workshop at her home. That event opened my eyes to how hungry people were for education on this subject, and served as confirmation for the direction I was feeling led to go. I'd also like to thank my friend Michelle Brill for encouraging me to write this book and inviting me to speak annually at the Palm Beach County Homeschool Expo. You opened significant doors, and I am grateful.

I'd also like to thank a few friends who proofread this book, my gracious friends, Rachel Hirsch, Sara Gates, Beth West, and Cindy Edgett. Thank you for your time and investment in this work.

Sometimes God sends you someone special to bless your life in ways you couldn't have imagined when you first met them. So it was with Lori Hatch. She was one of hundreds of neighbors who came to my home for a food forest tour. Lori and I struck up a conversation, swapped seeds, and became friends. Lori has been my most faithful prayer partner and supporter in this endeavor, giving an incredibly generous amount of time to help me grow in this space. I couldn't have done it without her. I wouldn't have wanted to try. Words can't express how grateful I am for her love and dedication. She's a gift.

Lastly, I need to thank my ever-so-patient and kind husband, Jared, and our precious sons, Lincoln, Harrison, and Levi. Thank you for sacrificing so that I could get this book out of my brain and onto paper. I pray that our world and your future will be better for it.

So, you want to plant a food forest.

How would you like a guide to help you with tips on what to do eight weeks out, six weeks out, one week out, and on planting day?

To get your free food forest installation checklist sent to you, sign up for our email list at

www.foodforestdiy.com

CONTENTS

INTRODUCTION

I want more people to get inspired and transform their yards. I know from experience; it'll be more than their yard that changes. I want people to reconsider the way they think about the green spaces around them, waking up to the reality that these aren't just for beauty and aesthetics, but they can also be practical and provide food for human flourishing. People are often intrigued by the idea of a 'food forest'. It's not terminology that's familiar, to be fair. What's wild to me is the impression that this food forest concept is "new" or trendy. This idea is the oldest in the book, the good book, that is. In the Bible, the book of Genesis tells us that humanity started in a forest garden named Eden.

For eons, people, just like you and me, grew their food. Imagine that was us. Imagine we had a connection to the earth and the land in a way that seems far from where we are now. Imagine we knew how to look up in the sky and tell what the weather was going to bring. Imagine we observed animal movement and patterns to help determine weather, seasons, and storms. Imagine our hearts were connected to the patch of earth we worked with our hands. Imagine we had a sense of place, meaning, and belonging, not just in the ethereal sense but also in the physical and material world. What if this became a reality for us? Do you think we'd be healthier for it? I imagine we'd be stronger in every sense – physically, spiritually, mentally, and emotionally.

Somewhere in recent history, we got disconnected. Modern inventions and mechanical conveniences meant we didn't need to grow our own food, and we could rely on big corporations and international supply chains to get food to us. We could trust that they were supplying us with fresh, clean food that was sustainably sourced… oh, wait. We can't trust that. We shouldn't. By now, clearly, we should all have a healthy dose of skepticism.

Transporting food across the globe to save a buck is not sustainable. If we can grow the food here rather than shipping it thousands of miles, shouldn't we? If we can design growing systems that hold water and carbon in a way that's regenerative to the soil and the ecosystem, why not? If we happened upon the oldest, simplest, most low-maintenance method for producing food, isn't it worth a shot?

I also wrote this book because the hour is urgent. The issues are at a critical point. We can see the signs of failing systems all around. With a world that's becoming increasingly out of control, growing food at home is one simple step to having peace of mind. Not only that, but it can become a part of the way we educate our children, giving them a broader understanding of the world and how it works. Food forest can be one element in giving them the gift of a childhood spent engaging with nature. Playing, getting dirty, exploring wild spaces. All this time outdoors can help bring calm to children with anxiety and ADHD. It can improve our minds, bodies, and souls.

With rising food costs, growing your produce can help lower grocery bills and be a hedge against inflation. There are a multitude of reasons to do this. In this book, I've set out to dare you to try, and give you the tools to help you find joy and satisfaction in growing your own food.

Important Note: to do the above, find joy and satisfaction in this endeavor, I'll need you to do something. Please. Do this for you. Check your perfectionism at the door. This is not going to be perfect. There will be bugs that eat leaves. There may not be enough rain, or there may be too much. You might kill a fruit tree. Take heart, my friend. Do you know how many fruit trees I've killed over the years? A lot. I've learned nearly every way to kill a fruit tree. At times, my chickens have helped. Wasn't that nice of them? They just couldn't help but dig up all the yummy dirt around my young avocado tree. Because I've made a lot of mistakes, I'll help you avoid pitfalls and be on the lookout for avoidable errors in planting that can have long-term consequences. But here's the heart of what I'm saying: this doesn't have to be perfect. It doesn't need to look like Joanna Gaines planted your food forest. There don't have to be café lights twinkling in the night. Let's be real – that would look amazing – but it's not an essential element to food forest. Not even close.

Don't compare yourself to me or anyone else. You're you. Your food forest is going to look and feel different from other people's. And that's okay. That's good. You are a distinctive person. You have a distinctive piece of land. You're going to create something unique. That's beautiful. I love that! I want you to love it, too, so remember that "comparison is the thief of joy." Don't fall for the trap.

It won't be perfect. Things will die. Do it anyway.

GLOSSARY OF TERMS

'Chop and drop' – this term refers to the practice of composting in place by cutting or pruning plants and dropping the plant material on the ground to let it serve as mulch and enrich the earth.

Corm – it's similar to a tuber or rhizome for the banana plant, which stores energy and sends out roots.

Cultivar/variety – select variations of a fruit tree; there are hundreds of mango cultivars – Orange Sherbet, Pineapple Pleasure, Coconut Cream, Fruit Cocktail – they're all mangoes, but with different flavors, growth habits, seasons in which they produce, degrees of pest/disease resistance, etc.

Cuttings – this refers to taking part of a stem (hardwood) or leaf (softwood) to create a new plant. Cuttings are most often rooted in soil or water, kept in shade until they have rooted and new growth has emerged.

Dappled sunlight – indirect sunlight that's filtered through the branches and leaves of mature trees. Picture sunlight coming through an oak tree.

Deciduous – trees or shrubs that lose their leaves annually; the subtropics they often look sad versus losing all leaves. The most common fruit tree referenced in this book that's deciduous is Mulberry.

Diva – this is the author's derogatory way of referring to a plant or fruit tree that is overly needy or has dramatic characteristics. This is a very official term that is *most definitely* found in all the horticultural literature.

Forage – can be used as a verb or noun; as a verb it means to look for wild edible plants, as a noun it means to produce food for livestock, similar to fodder.

Full shade – this refers to plants that can handle only a few hours of sunlight in the morning or late afternoon, or dappled sunlight all day, and can still produce in those conditions.

Full sun – this refers to plants that prefer six to eight hours of direct sun during the middle of the day.

Mother plant – a plant that is grown for the purpose of taking cuttings and propagating the plant.

Nitrogen-fixing – these plants can take nitrogen from the atmosphere, convert it into a form that plants can use, and put it into the soil, enriching the soil.

Nodes – the places on a stem where buds, leaves, and branches originate; nodes are important to locate especially when propagating plants, recognizing that both roots and new growth will emerge from the nodes. While pruning, this will influence where you make your cuts.

Part shade – this refers to a plant that prefers some protection from the sun, especially late in the day, needing shade from the sun in the western sky.

Propagate – this might be the most important term to learn if you want to build a food forest for free or cheap; propagation is the process of making new plants from existing ones, most easily done via seed or stem cutting.

CHAPTER 1
FOOD FOREST MOTIVATIONS & FOUNDATIONS

WHAT IS A FOOD FOREST?

A food forest is, at its simplest, an attempt to mimic nature, divine design. When you walk into a natural forest, there are multiple layers of growth. There are taller canopy trees, smaller 'understory' trees, bushes, shrubs, smaller plants, plants that grow along the ground, plants that make tubers or edible roots in the ground, and vines. Now imagine a part of your yard that incorporates all of these layers of growth, and every layer is producing food. That's a food forest. Imagine tall mango and avocado trees, smaller peach and cherry trees, bushes making mulberries, blackberries, beans, and leaf crops, alongside herbs like basil and oregano, with sweet potatoes creeping along the ground and passionfruit vines rambling up the trees, raining down fruit. Conceptually, that's a food forest! Now, add the benefit of growing food year-round. Congratulations! In most of Florida, we can do that. We can grow food all year long. Growing food in Florida also has unique challenges – intense heat, persistent pests, and sandy soil. But in my opinion, the benefits outweigh the challenges.

Many gardeners struggle needlessly in the subtropical climate because they're fighting nature trying to grow "Yankee vegetables" – what you find in grocery stores. Let's start with this: there are over 300,000 kinds of edible plants.[1] Only a smaller number of these are cultivated for commercial production and available on grocery store shelves. Those fruits and vegetables were not selected because they're the most delicious and most nutritious. They are commercially convenient to pack and ship. They have a thick skin and a long shelf life. Why are blackberries in the grocery store but not mulberries? Mulberries are sweeter than blackberries. They're healthier for you. They have more antioxidants. What mulberries don't have going for them is a long shelf life – the moment you pick them, they're ready to eat. These berries are not going to sit on a truck, train, or store shelf for several weeks and still look good. As a matter of fact, nothing I've picked fresh from my garden would've looked good a few weeks later. It makes you wonder

---

[1] https://www.bostonglobe.com/2023/05/04/magazine/there-are-300000-edible-plant-species-earth-why-do-we-eat-so-few-them/

what they do to food in the grocery store to keep it looking so good for so long.

MOTIVATIONS: ALL THE REASONS WHY

There are so many reasons: the education and formation of children, the gift of a low-maintenance growing method, our health – physical, mental, and spiritual, stewardship and sustainability, food security, and as a hedge against inflation. Most people have different reasons for wanting a food forest, and as they begin, they realize there are far more benefits than they initially realized. No matter what your personal motivation is, I want to help you realize the dream!

LOW-MAINTENANCE METHOD

The food forest concept is the easiest, most low-maintenance method of growing food. All other systems require more input and more work. This system incorporates many great practices: organic matter enriching the soil, retaining water, and nutrient cycling; the use of perennials for long-term sustainability; incorporating biodiversity (a wide variety of plants in close proximity) for pest resistance and resilience, and a food forest is beautiful, to boot. In a few pages, we'll discuss the differences between food forests, raised beds, orchards, and row gardens. You'll come to understand the reasons why this is the most low-maintenance system possible for producing food.

EDUCATION: FROM BACKYARD TO LIVING CLASSROOM

Children are like sponges. They're learning all the time, soaking up what they see and hear. We choose their environment and the kinds of things they're learning. Out in the food forest, children learn so much about nature and their surroundings, both the wildlife and plants that call the food forest home. One thing that becomes immediately apparent is the life cycle of plants. First comes a flower, then a fruit, then a seed, in that order. We can grow plants from seeds, but we can also propagate them from cuttings. The more you know, the more they'll know. They're watching you.

The average child in the US can identify up to 1,000 corporate logos but can't identify 10 native plants in the region where they live[2]. Most children and many adults can't tell the difference between the leaves of an Oak or a Maple. We've lost the basics. I want my children to be decent at leaf identification to a degree that is uncommon in their generation. And why not? These are real life skills that involve logic, pattern recognition, and fine motor skills. Not to mention the lessons that food forest offers on science, botany, nutrition, environmental science, and others. There's a lot to gain and nothing to lose by letting the food forest be a part of our educational plan for our children.

---

[2] https://www.psychologytoday.com/us/blog/why-the-wild-things-are/201304/nature-nurture

Having a food forest gets your children outside and creates an environment worth exploring. It invites butterflies and cool bugs. You'll find birds building nests in your trees. You might find the occasional tree frog hiding under a leaf. You're creating a fascinating world of wonder for your children to enjoy while learning about the birds, bugs, and reptiles they find. Help them learn to identify the different species of frogs, bugs, and birds for more educational opportunities.

A GARDEN TO CALL THEIR OWN

About a year ago my two oldest children told me that they wanted a garden bed of their own, so I gave them an area in my raised bed gardens. They helped weed the beds and decided what to plant in the garden. Not surprisingly, they wanted to plant broccoli and carrots. Not only are these their favorite veggies, but they are also fun to watch grow. Kids love harvesting carrots. Root crops are fun! I'd recommend giving your children a section of the food forest where they can plant whatever they want – flowers, veggies, herbs – it's up to them. As they learn to cultivate the ground and grow their own plants, they'll gain a sense of confidence and independence. And in a world that's grown increasingly loud, the garden can be a refuge. A place of quiet reflection where little people can pause long enough to think about things, to be curious, to wonder.

GIVE CHILDREN WORK

Children need chores. Joel Salatin reinforced this at the Florida Homeschool Convention in 2023. One of the major differences between children a hundred years ago and today is chores; morning chores, evening chores, farm chores, and house chores. Doing work gives children a sense of responsibility, purpose, and contribution. It gets them away from the lure of digital screens. Not only that, but psychologist Wendy Mogel said that "Helping out at home raises self-esteem: when parents insist that children do their chores, they are letting them know that they're not just loved, they are needed." The food forest provides ample opportunities for work, such as: pulling weeds, pruning plants, and spreading compost and mulch. These jobs are good for little bodies and little minds. Giving children an opportunity to develop a good work ethic and persistence builds character. We need to raise young people who know how to work, and work hard, reminding ourselves that they derive a sense of meaning, self-esteem, and satisfaction in their ability to accomplish tasks and do hard things.

LESSON IN ECONOMICS

Once your food forest is producing more food than you need, you can use the produce to trade or sell, or let your children start a little business and learn concepts of entrepreneurship. A few years ago, my then seven-year-old son, Lincoln, wanted to start a business. Since we had coconuts sprouting around the property, I suggested he start selling coconut palms. I gave him pots, dirt, and a shovel. He did the planting and asked if I could help with selling. Many folks would spend time shopping in my plant nursery at the end of my food forest tours. Lincoln would go out and talk with people about his coconut palms. He sold some! A motivated child could learn to propagate plants from seeds or cuttings and start a business. This would present opportunities to teach about managing money, business expenses, operating costs, wholesale pricing, savings, and more.

A HEDGE AGAINST INFLATION

Having a food forest can positively affect your grocery bill. Food prices increased 20% between 2018 and 2022.[3] We all could use help feeding our families better quality food at lower prices. Despite initial costs, a food forest will continue to provide food indefinitely. Imagine harvesting fresh fruits, organic greens, and tropical potatoes year-round, year after year. In 2020 we saw what kinds of shortages can happen when disruption impacts the supply chain. Even more recently, the price of eggs more than doubled in early 2023 due to an avian flu outbreak. That sticker shock made those of us who own chickens feel pretty good about our investment in homegrown poultry. Keeping chickens is always a good idea, wink wink.

---

[3] https://www.ers.usda.gov/data-products/ag-and-food-statistics-charting-the-essentials/food-prices-and-spending/?topicId=1afac93a-444e-4e05-99f3-53217721a8be

SELF-SUFFICIENCY AND FOOD SECURITY

According to the Smithsonian, in 1945, nearly fifty percent of Americans were growing food in their backyard gardens, and collectively they produced forty percent of all the produce in the United States.[4] That generation had the knowledge and skills to achieve this feat. They were more resilient, and at least, partially self-sufficient. They knew how to "do the stuff" and cultivate the ground to produce healthy food for their families. Since that time just a few generations ago, grocery stores and delivery services are so convenient that we've been lulled to sleep. The average American could not feed their family on their own for any meaningful length of time, making them dependent on big corporations, fragile supply chains, and the federal government. To make matters worse, many Americans have also lost the knowledge and skills to cultivate the land and feed themselves, making us all both less resilient and less free.

It has not always been this way. It does not have to be this way. We can change it. We can regain the knowledge and skills of our grandparents' generation to become more self-sufficient and to become better stewards of the earth, just like those who came before us.

Any student of history or even of the current armed conflicts in places like Central Africa, Syria, and Yemen can attest to the reality that food is a significant issue in war and is sometimes

---

[4] https://gardens.si.edu/gardens/victory-garden/

weaponized. You may have heard the adage "Control the food, control the people." I don't want to be subject to the whims of wars and tyrants. I don't know whether we'll have any more pandemics or disruptions in the supply chain, but I'd like to think that if we did, I could feed my family. It's not the job of grocery stores or the government to feed my children, it's my job. And to the degree that I can do that with what I have, I will.

GOOD FOR THE BODY: IMPACTS ON PHYSICAL HEALTH

What's being sprayed on our produce? What chemicals are in the plastic our food comes packaged in? Carcinogens? Endocrine disruptors? Are hormone levels being affected? Concerns about the food systems produced by Big Agriculture abound. These are fair questions, and often we can't know for sure. The best way to know without a doubt that your food hasn't been sprayed with harmful chemicals or processed in a way that brings adverse health effects is to grow it yourself. If you didn't grow the food, and you don't personally know the farmer who grew the food, you do not know how your food was produced. Period. Not only is growing food yourself more gratifying, but you also know for certain that it's safe and clean.

Beyond whatever chemical pesticides and fertilizers are being used, the nutritional quality of produce today is greatly diminished due to a steep loss of soil fertility. What happens when you farm on the same land for a hundred years, relying on chemicals to make things grow? The soil gets worse and worse. It's not rich and black, full of worms and life. It's more like dust. That's what's been happening in America's farmlands, due to over-farming, erosion, and a failure to engage in regenerative practices.

What happens when you grow broccoli or tomatoes in poor quality soil? What happens when you grow those same vegetables in rich, black dirt? Will one taste better than the other? Will it have more nutrients? More minerals? Yes, yes, and yes. Have you ever wondered why the food you grew yourself tastes better? There are several reasons, but one is soil quality. When you grow vegetables in rich soil, using organic matter to build the soil and act as fertilizer, of course, that produce will taste better than produce grown in dust, sprayed with chemical fertilizers to make them grow. The other factor is the stage of maturity at which the produce is picked. Because of the time it takes to transport, many tomatoes on grocery store shelves were picked green and then gassed to ripen. A tomato picked early does not have the same nutrition as one that ripens on the vine.

GOOD FOR THE MIND; IMPACTS ON MENTAL HEALTH

It should be intuitively understood that being outside is good for you, and it is, but there's more. The divine designer is so brilliant, that even dirt is good for us and has healing properties. Soil has a mycobacterium in it that triggers the release of the happy hormones, dopamine, and serotonin[5]. Getting dirt stuck under your fingernails will make you happier and less stressed! Spending time out in the sun, surrounded by nature, playing in the dirt can fight mild anxiety and depression.

Spending time in the food forest also lowers cortisol. Multiple studies have confirmed that being in a natural environment is good to reduce stress. In Britain, doctors are prescribing this to patients; they refer to it as "horticultural therapy." It's the reality that spending time in nature is good for you. In one study, the researchers had two groups – one group of people walked through an urban area, and the other walked through a natural area. At the end of the walk, they measured their cortisol levels.[6] I'll give you one guess who was less stressed. The folks who walked though a park, of course!

For children and adults with ADHD, being outside is even more beneficial. More time in nature reduces restlessness and hyperactivity. It increases concentration, lowers stress, and increases sensory regulation. Overall, the natural environment provides a range of therapeutic benefits for people with ADHD, supporting their cognitive, emotional, and physical well-being. Integrating outdoor activities into their routines can aid existing

---

[5] https://permaculture.com.au/why-gardening-makes-you-happy-and-cures-depression/#:~:text=Getting%20your%20hands%20dirty%20in%20the%20garden%20can,a%20natural%20anti-depressant%20and%20strengthens%20the%20immune%20system.

[6] https://www.sciencedirect.com/science/article/abs/pii/S1618866720307494

strategies for managing ADHD symptoms and improve overall quality of life. There is a common saying among gardeners, "A little dirt never hurt!"

If there's ever a generation that needs to feel connected to the Earth, it's this one. Back in the spring of 2020, only a few months into COVID, I met a young man who was struggling with crippling anxiety, and no wonder, he'd been locked away in his apartment, spending most of his life on screens. He was standing on the street in front of my home, talking with me as I watered my watermelon patch. He had become depressed and said, "I don't feel connected to the material world." I motioned to my food forest and said, "Come, grab a shovel. Let's dig up some yuca." And we did. As he dug, we talked about the meaning of life, the universe, and truth. It was an opportunity to explore big ideas while doing a simple thing. He took the cassava home, looked up recipes, and started baking. Over time, he started experimenting with recipes using other food forest crops. He came up with the most incredible dessert recipes you could think of. Cassava Cheesecake and Purple Yam pie were some of my favorites. If we can get our children off screens when they're young, get them outside, and foster a sense of connection with nature, that'll do a lot to promote their mental health long-term.

GOOD FOR THE SOUL; IMPACTS ON SPIRITUAL HEALTH

Growing food increases our sense of awe and wonder at creation. I've many epiphanies in the food forest. The teachings of Jesus come alive as you watch things grow. John 12:24 says "Unless a kernel of wheat falls to the ground and dies, it remains only a seed; but if it dies, it bears much fruit." This verse speaks to the reality that by dying to ourselves we can produce the fruit of the Spirit, "love, joy, peace, patience, kindness, goodness, faithfulness, gentleness, and self-control."

As you spend time working with plants, watching them go from flower to fruit to seed, the parables start to make sense. Jesus was speaking to an agrarian society, which is why many Biblical stories use symbols and analogies from farming. Jesus said that if we had faith the size of a mustard seed, which is the smallest of all seeds, we could move mountains. In John 15, Jesus said "I am the true vine, and my Father is the gardener. He cuts off every branch in me that bears no fruit, while every branch that does bear fruit he prunes so that it will be even more fruitful." In this metaphor, Jesus presents Himself as the vine, and God the Father as the gardener. Through this pruning and refining process, we become more fruitful.

One of the most famous farming stories Jesus told is commonly referred to as the "parable of the sower" from Luke 8.

Jesus told this parable: "A farmer went out to sow his seed. As he was scattering the seed, some fell along the path; it was trampled on, and the birds ate it up. Some fell on rocky ground, and when it came up, the plants withered because they had no moisture. Other seed fell among thorns, which grew up with it and choked the plants. Still other seed fell on good soil. It came up and yielded a crop, a hundred times more than was sown."

When he said this, he called out, "Whoever has ears to hear, let them hear."

His disciples asked him what this parable meant. He said, "The knowledge of the secrets of the kingdom of God has been given to you, but to others I speak in parables, so that,

"'though seeing, they may not see;
though hearing, they may not understand.'

"This is the meaning of the parable: The seed is the word of God. Those along the path are the ones who hear, and then the devil comes and takes away the word from their hearts, so that they may not believe and be saved. Those on the rocky ground are the ones who receive the word with joy when they hear it, but they have no root. They believe for a while, but in the time of testing they fall away. The seed that fell among thorns stands for those who hear, but as they go on their way they are choked by life's worries, riches and pleasures, and they do not mature. But the seed on good soil stands for those with a noble

and good heart, who hear the word, retain it, and by
persevering produce a crop."

The food forest is a great place to talk to God, process pain, and seek wisdom. As it says in Romans 1:18-20, there's a lot of truth hidden in plain sight.

GOOD FOR THE EARTH: A MORE SUSTAINABLE MODEL

Food Forest answers environmental concerns on many levels. The food forest concept with a strong leaf or mulch layer, traps more carbon than any other method, thus reducing greenhouse gases. It promotes soil health which enhances nutrient cycling and water retention, reducing run-off and erosion. This is a more efficient use of water than monoculture farming. When a region is struggling with drought, any method of growing food that requires less water is a winner! Food forests incorporate biodiversity and create habitat for wildlife; especially pollinators like birds, bees, and butterflies, all of whom are essential to a healthy ecosystem. Most folks building food forests compost their kitchen scraps, which greatly reduces the amount of waste going into landfills. I'm personally convinced that God hates waste; as it's an indication of poor stewardship. Why buy compost or good dirt when we could make it ourselves with items we intended to throw away?

The more food we produce ourselves, the less we buy from big corporations, who import the produce from all over the globe.

Next time you're in the grocery store produce section, pay attention to the country of origin. I sometimes shop at Costco. In the produce section I was stunned to see where the tropical fruit was coming from: keep in mind, all of these can grow here. Watermelon from Costa Rica, Papaya from Mexico, Pineapple from Guatemala, and Tangerines from Morocco. My mind was blown! Our tangerines were grown in North Africa and shipped thousands of miles across the Atlantic. That's nuts. How much fuel did they burn in transport? How much did it cost in labor and supplies? What was the effect on our earth? Why are we shipping things around the globe when they could be locally sourced? This is not to mention the boon that would come to local economies if all of us shifted our buying dollars from Walmart to the farmer's market. Small is beautiful. Growing food locally reduces carbon emissions, strengthens local economies, and makes your community more resilient. When supply chains are disrupted, the local economy is all you've got. Let's build it now. Let's support it now. Food security is freedom, and it's good for the earth.

STEWARDSHIP OF YOUR EDEN

The Garden of Eden account records that humanity was mandated to be stewards of the earth. Another word for steward is 'manager.' When I talk to young children, I'll ask, "How do you think we should manage your backyard? Should we grow grass, or should we grow food?" Every child shouts excitedly

"Food! Food!" It's intuitive to kindergartners that growing food is the best stewardship of their yard. What's obvious to five-year-olds is lost on many adults. The problem for us, grownups in the West, is that we've been conditioned to the American dream. A neat house with a white picket fence, a perfect grass lawn, and if you want privacy, 120 of the same plants in a line. Where did we learn this? It's not the most beautiful option, or the most beneficial. Most of our hedge plants don't flower or fruit. What is there about all the grass and non-flowering hedges to attract bees and butterflies? To feed birds? What is there about these thousands of dollars of landscape plants that can sustain you, the wildlife, or life on earth? Very little.

Most people don't spend time thinking about it, but the whole idea of grass lawns is a bit weird. There are ground cover plants that would do a much better job, requiring no maintenance and little water. These plants produce flowers for pollinators and are nitrogen-fixing, fertilizing the soil. Forget grass. Save several hours of work a week. Stop employing your lawn people and plant ground covers instead. You'll save tens of thousands of dollars throughout your life while benefiting pollinators and enriching the soil. I call that a win-win!

Grass is the most pointless agricultural product. You pay thousands of dollars to buy it, install it, water it, and cut it. Then you harvest it and throw it away. This is lunacy. This is wasteful. In the third world, this would be considered a luxury any day of the week. The time for luxury and vanity is over. The time for practicality is here. Embrace the new normal. Grow your own food. Join the rebellion!

EVERYONE, JOIN THE REVOLUTION!

Back in the 1960s, rebellion against societal norms looked like partying, using drugs, listening to music their parents didn't appreciate, and refusing to conform or settle down in suburbia. Times have changed. If you had told someone back then what rebellion looks like today, they wouldn't have believed you. Being a rebel today against what's normal in our culture now looks quite different. It looks like getting married, having children, buying land, growing food, and learning to take care of yourself. That's the way we resist what ails our society. Our society is sick – physically, emotionally, and spiritually. There's something about getting out into open spaces and creating a world for your children handcrafted by you. They can have a carefree childhood of innocence, but we must fight for it.

Who should grow a food forest? Anyone! Everyone! Anyone with land, and even people who don't own land are finding a way! Petition your local landowners including churches, schools, HOA's, public parks, etc. There are vacant lots and spaces on the margins of properties that would make excellent food forests. Believe it or not, many churches are joining this bandwagon, and some are leading the way! In my town, I know of at least four churches that have started food forests and community gardens. Often, all it takes is for someone to step up and volunteer to lead the program. Often, the church may have room in the budget for startup costs; or you might find a local landscape company or nursery willing to donate materials. Get creative! I know of churches hosting gardening workshops as a part of their belief in preparedness. I even know of a church that built large-scale greenhouse gardens and processing plants so that once the food is produced, it can be made into jams, jellies, and salsas. If you're a part of a church, get involved! Consider approaching the leaders requesting to use a portion of the church land to grow food. This concept was birthed in the Garden of Eden, and spiritual leaders will see that if you give them the chance. And hey, if all else fails, get them a copy of this book! My company, Food Forest DIY, would be happy to help them design an aesthetically pleasing space that also produces food. Let's get back to Eden.

LEARNING LOCALLY

The first step is educating yourself on what grows in your zone. Reading this book is a good start, but if you're not in Florida, you'll want to start consuming content from folks growing food nearby. YouTube, podcasts, books, whatever your preferred method of learning is, there's plenty of great content creators aiming to teach people the basics of growing food in your zone.

Get down to an even more micro level. Are there people in your neighborhood doing this? Start to observe when you drive around. Do you see any fruit trees? Any gardens? Maybe start a

Facebook page for your neighborhood for people interested in food forest. Ask a question on Nextdoor, "Hey, neighbors! I'm interested in starting a food forest and looking for people who want to learn together. If you're doing the same, let's talk!" You could have different neighbors give you a tour of their yard, you give a tour of yours, and swap cuttings and seeds.

One of the best (and free!) ways to build a food forest is to learn about plant propagation. There are so many plants that you can start from cuttings or seeds. A cutting is when you take a piece of a branch, put it in a pot, and it roots – growing a new plant! Now, just do that one hundred more times and you've got a plant nursery! I'm kidding… but for real, that's sort of how it happens.

I had many neighbors who shared cuttings and seeds with me to help me get started. In turn, for many years I hosted complimentary food forest tours and gave away tons of cuttings and seeds. It was my way of investing in my community; teaching skills that I had learned and sharing from the bounty that the land produced.

CHAPTER 2
FOOD FOREST DESIGN & BASICS

DIFFERENT THAN AN ORCHARD

In an orchard, rows of trees are planted at uniform spacing between each tree and row. Typically, the space between the trees is not utilized. There might be grass, native plants, weeds, and a leaf layer. Often pesticides are sprayed to kill weeds. In a food forest, the space between the trees is filled with useful plants. Leaf crops, nitrogen-fixing beans, root crops, and flowering herbs, to name a few. There is a wide variety of crops that could fill the space, especially while the fruit trees are young and there is plenty of light. In permaculture, this is called a fruit tree "guild". These are plants that work together to benefit the system: some fix nitrogen, attract pollinators, deter pests, reduce erosion, serve as a windbreak, and accumulate mulch/leaf litter for nutrient cycling. This is the power of biodiversity in action.

DIFFERENT THAN A RAISED BED OR ROW GARDEN

Traditional gardening methods using annual crops is labor intensive. Many of these plants produce in 60 to 90 days, which means you're re-seeding and planting new crops every two to three months. This is a fine way to produce food, if you have the time and resources necessary to replant frequently, fight off pests, and keep them looking 'pretty.' In my experience, annual vegetables are much more susceptible to pests and disease than perennials. They also have a limited season due to our warm climate.

Perennials are the lazy gardener's best friend. You plant them once, and they produce forever.

Note: Some of the plants suggested here are what would be considered short-term perennials, which means they grow for much longer than an annual, but might die back after anywhere from 18 months to several years. Long-term perennials keep producing indefinitely.

I'll say one more thing here. As a culture, we've become obsessed with perfection and aesthetics, and I think it's high time to reconsider that. What if we rewilded a part of our yard? What if we gave it back to nature? What if we planted fruit trees, edible things, and allowed the native plants to grow? You'd get something like a wild food forest, with medicinal natives and pollinators mixed in. I think that kind of system is wise on a lot of levels. One thing many people never consider is that if our region were to face difficult times, for whatever reason, and people became hungry, a raised bed or row garden would be raided in short order. Everyone knows what tomatoes look like. How nice of you to plant them all in a row! I've heard that hornworms think similarly. But, imagine a wild food forest, where food and non-edible natives grow together. Where some of the leaves are edible and some are toxic. Can most Americans accurately identify Katuk or Chaya? No. I've considered incorporating complex crops to sabotage looting efforts and deter theft. Jicama makes a good candidate for this. Despite having a tasty root, Jimaca makes toxic beans. Eat them, and you'll wish you hadn't. There's something about growing food in a forest system that offers resilience and protection, not just against wind and cold, but also against pests and looters. As uncertainty in our world continues to mount, the ability of the food forest model to protect itself is an advantage to your family's food security. Like many things, food forest rewards knowledge and punishes ignorance. It should be noted that the ideal plan is to be surrounded by like-minded people who band together, turn lawns into farms, and help each other. Fingers crossed.

WHERE TO PLANT YOUR FOOD FOREST

Think about your property. Depending on the amount of space, you've got land immediately adjacent to your home. Then you've got land a little further out. Then you've got land on the perimeter, near fences, hedges, and roads. Let's call the land immediately next to your house zone one. The land a little further out is zone two. The land on the perimeter is zone three.

I have two suggestions depending on how much land you have. For things you'll use in the kitchen often, like herbs and greens, plant in zone one. You may not want to walk across half an acre to get a little basil. The other good option is to plant heavily in zone three along the perimeter, depending on how much land you own. Many people want to keep some open space in their yards which is understandable. On my two-acre property, I planted herbs and greens close to my back door, with fruit trees along the north side and perimeter of the property. One permaculture principle is to "use edges and value the marginal." Just because the perimeter of the property is a marginal amount of space, doesn't mean it's not useful. Often, that space wasn't being utilized anyway, so why not use it to grow food?

HOW MUCH LAND?

This depends on how many fruit trees are included and how much space you want to give them. I've created designs for food banks that at maturity would produce 10,000 pounds of food on a quarter acre. It's entirely possible to do a lot with a little. A tenth of an acre of growing space would suffice for the average family of four. Here's some grandmotherly wisdom: use what you've got. Whatever earth you have access to, use it. Your children will play and have adventures in the food forest to be sure. Building forts, catching critters, snacking on fruit, and enjoying fragrant blooms are just a few things to do for fun. Who remembers the book *The Secret Garden*? There's something about densely planted foliage that creates a world of magic and wonder in which young minds can feel independent and explore. I would also consider incorporating benches, swings, and bird baths to make the food forest a welcoming and enjoyable space.

DIRECTIONAL DESIGN

Here's the general rule: plant tall trees on the north side, and the best sun is on the south side. All properties are different, and this can be applied to any patch of earth you're working with. Imagine you've got a square that's 20 feet by 20 feet. In that square, you want to plant four fruit trees at the four corners. You're planting two tall mangoes, and two starfruits. Starfruit won't be nearly as tall as mango. You'd want to plant the mango north of the starfruit, so that as the tree grows, it doesn't shade out the starfruit. For most plants, too much shade equals decreased flowering and fruiting. For this reason, I generally recommend that you keep all fruit trees in a food forest pruned to 10-15 feet, so you can reach the fruit, and keep the food forest canopy open. If one tree gets huge, it will shade out others, and you won't get as much fruit.

DIE, GRASS, DIE

You might be horrified at the idea of removing grass, but to create a true food forest with all the layers, removing grass is essential. You can build your food forest in one large area, on smaller islands, or in syntropic rows. Any way you do it, the first step is to remove grass.

There's a couple of ways to do this. If you're short on time, you could rent a sod cutter from Home Depot. It's a heavy machine that cuts sod at whatever depth you set it to, usually two to three inches deep is all you need. This process is labor intensive. Sod is heavy to lift, and once you have it all removed, it'll fill the back of a pickup truck and you need somewhere to dump it. If you have ample time before you begin your project, you could try killing the grass via solarization. Take a tarp or visqueen and cover the grass. Put bricks, rocks, or something heavy on the corners so the tarp doesn't get blown away by wind. If you can keep the grass covered for six to eight weeks, you can usually kill it within that period of time. This should also kill any nematodes present in the soil. From there, the grass will be easier to remove because it's dried up.

Note about noxious weeds that can't be deterred by solarization and sod cutting. There are a few weeds that are the stuff of nightmares. Torpedograss, Nutsedge, and Wedelia are all truly terrible in their own rights, and extremely difficult to eradicate. Some have tubers and runners deep in the ground. You'll have to excavate to remove them. Do some due diligence to make sure you don't have these growing in your yard. Nearly everyone in the landscaping world will tell you that trying to remove them mechanically followed by Roundup is the only way to get rid of them. Eek. Besides a shovel and a lot of work, I don't have a better idea. Whenever you're removing, you must get the roots. Pulling up the plant does zero good unless you have the roots and the runners; this is especially true with Torpedograss.

HELP! MY LAND IS SAND

Welcome to Florida. It's sandy, alkaline soil. It's not just you, it's everyone. That's why we're fanatics about chop and drop, using compost, manure, mulching, and planting crops that are known to thrive in a subtropical sandy environment. When you grow what grows here, you experience more joy and less frustration in your gardening efforts.

USING MULCH AS A LEAF LAYER

In building a food forest, we use copious amounts of mulch. Mulch serves at least three functions: it holds moisture, suppresses weeds, and over time, breaks down into rich soil. If you don't have irrigation, mulch is even more essential. Think about the way a sponge holds water. That's what mulch does for your plants, keeping the ground wet longer, protecting the soil from the baking sun, keeping the weeds at bay, and eventually breaking down into nutrient-rich dirt. There's no downside. We use mulch to mimic the leaf layer that's found on the natural forest floor. Notice next time you are in the woods, if you walk off the trail under the tree canopy, the ground often feels squishy or spongy. It has some give. It's not hard-packed. If you kick back the top leaves, you'll find rich, black earth that's teeming with life, full of worms and grubs and other living things. The soil is alive because for the last several decades, leaves have been falling, blanketing the ground and eventually, they break down. This continues year after year, creating a thick leaf layer that holds moisture and becomes rich soil. We want to do the same thing in our food forest. Hence, mulch!

Everyone asks: what kind of mulch? Anything will do except dyed mulch. We're growing food, so you don't want wood that's been dyed a different color. Rubber mulch is also out of the question. As a gardener, I'm offended that this stuff exists in the first place.

In my area, it's easy to get a dump truck full of wood chips, but not every property is suited for that. You're usually talking about a space that's at least ten feet wide by twelve to twenty feet long. Imagine a mulch pile six feet high filling that entire space. Bigger trucks = bigger space.

Bagged mulch is much easier to move around the yard unless you don't mind a sore back from hours and hours loading mulch into wheelbarrows with a pitchfork. The most accessible bagged mulch in my area is Cypress Mulch or Pine Bark, either one is fine. If you're on a budget, and you have Oak trees, or you know someone who does, go rake up their leaves. Field tests have demonstrated that when they break down, oak leaves have the same pH as mulch.[7] They'll work just as well. If you're lucky, wait until oak leaves are falling in Florida, usually between November and January. Your neighbors will do this really nice thing. They'll rake up all their leaves, bag them up for you, and put them out to the road for easy pickup. How kind!

Pro tip: if you're trying to keep citrus alive, which in many cases is an effort in futility eventually doomed to fail, oak leaves are especially helpful. There's a theory that oak and citrus have a symbiotic and mutually beneficial relationship. While most orange groves in Florida are riddled with a myriad of diseases despite intense spraying, there are beautiful disease-free orange trees in the old oak forests around Brooksville and other parts of Florida. Why are they clean and productive, while the commercial production groves are diseased? One theory that deserves merit: oaks. One way that I trick my citrus trees into thinking there's an oak nearby is by making an oak leaf compost tea. Fill a five-gallon bucket with oak leaves and water. Let it sit for at least a week. Longer is better. Then, use the water on your

---

[7] https://yardandgarden.extension.iastate.edu/faq/can-oak-leaves-be-used-garden-mulch#:~:text=Yes.%20While%20oak%20leaves%20are%20slightly%20acidic%2C%20an,should%20have%20little%20effect%20on%20the%20soil%20pH.

citrus trees. Viola! They think an oak is nearby. Yay for tricking nature into submission.

Note: when mulching citrus, be mindful that they have aerial roots. You'll want to keep mulch back at least 6-12 inches away from the trunk, so those aerial roots can breathe.

In food forest, there's this concept called "chop and drop" which means that as we prune plants, we leave the branches and leaves on the forest of the food forest to help build up the leaf layer. They will rot and compost in place. This makes sense, right? Why would we bring in oak leaves and mulch, but then haul out leaves that the food forest put energy into producing?

COVER THE GROUND

As the mulch breaks down over time, it's vitally important that we also plant a ground cover. In food forests, we often use nitrogen-fixing ground covers like Sunshine Mimosa or Perennial Peanut. These plants are beneficial as both pollinators and nitrogen-fixers, improving the soil. You'd want to plant them a maximum of eight feet apart, or even closer together, so they nicely fill the space.

Some local municipalities are getting with the program and are moving away from planting grass. I'm starting to see Perennial Peanut being used in medians and other roadway landscaping. And why not? Why wouldn't you want a no-maintenance solution? These plants will stay low. You'll never need to mow.

They flower, feeding bees and butterflies. They are nitrogen-fixing, naturally improving the soil. Grass seems like such a loser proposition now, doesn't it? There's only one thing worse: turf. I'm kidding, but I'm not kidding. I understand that it has its place, in small yards and places where it's so shady that grass won't grow. But please, don't ask the garden girl if she likes turf, or any fake plant, really. She doesn't.

One fun thing to note about Sunshine Mimosa – not only does it produce pink powderpuff blooms, it also responds to touch. This plant has commonly been called 'sensitive plant', 'shy plant', or 'touch-me-not'. The fern-like leaves on this plant recoil and fold up in response to wind or touch. Kids love to watch this!

HEDGEROWS: A FOOD FOREST ALIGNED ALTERNATIVE

There's this British concept called a Hedgerow. Rather than planting dozens of the same plant, imagine that we chose five different plants, and planted them in clumps. You'd get plants that flowered and fruited at different times. You could mix in edible plants, medicinal plants, pollinators, and ornamentals. Imagine a Hedgerow with clumps of Elderberry, making beautiful white flowers and then medicinal berries in the Fall. Then, you could have a section of Pigeon Pea, with yellow blooms that flower in winter, then making beans. The plants are also fixing nitrogen and improving the soil. You could also include cherries like Grumichama or Cherry of the Rio Grande that flower in spring. These are easily hedged and produce edible fruit. For the butterflies, you could add pollinators like Firebush, Firespike, Pentas, and Lantana. For aromatics, you could use Sweet Almond or Radermachera (Tree Jasmine). These hedgerows could be much more beautiful, colorful, and productive than the standard boring hedge. I promise.

BUSY BEES ARE ESSENTIAL

Did you know that in parts of the world they've sprayed bees into extinction? Shocking, I know. In the Sichuan Province, located in southwest China, they now have to hand-pollinate millions of acres of apple and pear orchards.[8] I kid you not. They sprayed so many pesticides so thoughtlessly for so long that there are no more bees. Air pollution and habitat loss contributed to the catastrophe. Can you imagine? No bees! Say goodbye to one-third of the foods you enjoy eating.

Here in the US, more than 70 species of pollinators are endangered. 25% of America's bumble bees are at risk of extinction. The rusty patched bumblebee, which used to inhabit North Dakota and Minnesota, was last seen in 2003.[9] We need to do everything we can to make a hospitable environment for

---

[8] https://www.foodunfolded.com/article/pollinating-orchards-by-hand-lessons-from-sichuan-china

[9] https://www.trvst.world/biodiversity/endangered-pollinators-conservation/#:~:text=The%20U.S.%20Fish%20and%20Wildlife%20Service%20says,more%20than%2070%20species%20of%20pollinators%20are%20endangered.

bees, both at a governmental level and at a personal level. Bees are essential to life on earth.

Building a food forest creates a habitat for pollinators. Consider incorporating pollinator plants in your food forest shrub layer. Some of my favorites include Powderpuff (*Calliandra haematocephala* which is the bush variety, not the tree form), Butterfly Bush, Firebush, Jamaican Caper, Crepe Myrtle, Buttonbush, Texas Sage, and Lantana. We're too far south to grow Azaleas, but if I were in a region where they'd thrive, Azaleas would make my list!

SYNTROPIC ROWS FOR SMALL YARDS

For people with small yards, this is one of the best uses of space. Syntropic agriculture is a concept coming out of Brazil, where you still plant orchard-style, but utilize the space between the trees to grow useful crops. The way this works in small yards is by selecting an area where there is some space, but not a ton. You pick an area that's at least five to six feet wide by however many feet long. Let's say it's 40 feet long. We want to plant a dwarf mango, avocado, and jackfruit. Remember the principle: plant tall trees on the north side. Out of these, the tallest will be jackfruit. So, if this row is oriented north to south, jackfruit goes on the north side. Also, remember that jackfruit only needs about ten feet in between trees. Mango and avocado need about 15 feet. So, I'd orient it like this from north to south – jackfruit, avocado, mango – keeping attractive tree specimens on the ends, with the least attractive tree hidden in the middle. Avocados make great fruit, but depending on the variety, they aren't always pretty.

In between the trees, we'd plant things like yuca, chaya, and katuk for the shrub layer. Then, around the fruit trees, we'd build guilds. These are helpful plants; they help each other, and the tree. Plants like Brazilian sissoo spinach, African blue basil, comfrey, and marigolds. I'd be planting anything that needs shade from the western sun a bit behind the young tree, to the east side. This is the area that will be shaded by the tree in the afternoon.

PATHWAYS & EDGING

There are various opinions on whether these are necessary. Pathways aren't a necessity, but they are lovely. I've seen them done well with both gravel and pine bark. If you use mulch in the food forest, but then the path is pine bark, it's pretty obvious where the pathway is. For folks who are trying to be economical, I'd recommend spending funds on fruit trees and other plants if your budget is limited. Edging is a bit more of a necessity, especially if your food forest is surrounded by grass. You want a barrier to keep the grass from growing back into your food forest, and it's good to have something to weed whack against. Some folks use railroad ties, landscape lumber, logs, pavers, or plastic edging to line their food forest. Another 'use what you've got' inspired idea is to cut down bamboo or areaca poles if you have them in your yard. Lay them lengthwise and you've got a border.

CHAPTER 3
STAPLE CROPS RULE

Lots of people think they have a food forest when in reality, they have an orchard. A bunch of fruit trees does not make a food forest. I've heard it said that in tough times, if you want to keep people going, give them an egg and a potato every day. I can't ensure you get chickens, which is always a good idea, but growing potatoes and high protein greens is a no-brainer. Not only are they calorie crops, food that can feed people nearly year-round, but they're also cheap, much cheaper than fruit trees, and easy to propagate.

In the subtropics, our staple crops are tropical potatoes, bananas, beans, and greens that are high in protein. These four elements should be included in every food forest whenever possible. And redundancy is key. Don't bet the farm on one crop. Plant multiple kinds of tropical potatoes, high protein greens, and other calorie crops. There's a saying from the Navy Seals that speaks to the power of redundancy, *"Two is one. One is none."* If one crop fails, you have others. If one fruit tree dies, you planted a second. Go for redundancy.

TROPICAL POTATOES

There are four primary root crops that do well in the subtropics. They are yuca, yams, sweet potatoes, and tubers in the malanga/taro family. They each grow differently, and I'll cover them individually.

YUCA MAKES THE WORLD GO ROUND

Manihot esculenta

Cassava/yuca is the number one root crop grown in the subtropics worldwide. Last year, 300 million tons of cassava were produced to make cassava flour and other foods. Cassava is about twice as productive as wheat on the same amount of land.[10] There's a good reason that cassava is grown by subsistence farmers around the world. It's drought tolerant and can perform well even in poor soil. It's a good source of carbohydrates. Cassava leaves are edible when cooked and are a rich source of protein, minerals, and vitamins.

Cassava grows like a tall, woody plant. You make more plants from stem cuttings. This plant is exponential – from one plant this year, you could make ten plants next year. From ten plants,

---

[10] https://en.wikipedia.org/wiki/Cassava#Production

you could make one hundred plants. From one hundred plants, you could make one thousand. Talk about food security. You could feed a whole neighborhood with this stuff, so long as all the neighbors were willing to work their land. This is resilience.

Cassava should be planted in early spring after the danger of frost has passed and harvested in late fall. I usually plant in March and harvest in December, give or take a few weeks. You can also stagger your planting and harvesting over a few months, but as a general rule, plant before the rainy season. Cassava should be planted in a full sun location, spaced about four feet apart from each other and heavily mulched. Because you're trying to grow thick roots, you don't want weeds or grass competing for nutrients in the soil. Also, where you grow cassava should be rotated every year. If you continue to grow cassava on the same piece of land year after year without rotating the crop, production will drop by two-thirds.[11]

Because there's space around the cassava, this is an opportunity for intercropping. You'd want to intercrop with something you don't mind digging up ten months later. An annual in the bean family would be excellent, as they are nitrogen-fixing. Cowpea, also called black-eyed peas, would work well. You should fertilize cassava every four to six weeks through the rainy season. Good organic options would be compost, manure, coffee grounds, bone meal, blood meal, fish emulsion, or seaweed

[11] https://biblio.iita.org/documents/S17InbkKuyperIntercroppingNothomNodev.pdf-a2205c618fc1ecce13d043c879e43b6a.pdf

extract. You want nitrogen. If getting an inorganic NPK fertilizer, use something like 15-15-15.

When harvesting, dig up cassava roots as you need them. If you just need two roots to make some fries for dinner, then just dig up two roots, not the entire plant. Cassava roots do not store well. Once dug, you must use or freeze within three days. The best way to store them is by leaving them in the ground, connected to the plant. This works for up to six months. If left too long after you should have harvested, the roots will become tough and woody.

As you harvest a few roots at a time, eventually you'll dig up the whole plant. That's how it works! Just keep the plant in your garage or lean it up against a fence for a few weeks or months until you're ready to replant. Do not cut into smaller pieces until replanting. I cut cassava stems into ten to twelve inch long pieces with at least five nodes. The thicker the cutting, the stronger the plant will be.

Peeling cassava requires some knowledge. The first time I tried to peel cassava, I used a peeler. That's how you peel potatoes, right? Hilariously and dangerously wrong! If you want to spend all day trying to peel a cassava and perhaps injure yourself, use a peeler. I finally watched a YouTube video from an African farmer on how to peel a cassava. It was so easy! You take a knife, and cut into the cassava about an eighth of an inch, making a line down the center from top to bottom. Two layers of skin peel back, a brown layer, and a white or pink layer, depending on the variety. Remove those and you're ready to use it however you'd like. Note that down the center of a cassava root is a thin vein of woody stem. I usually remove those before cooking but some prefer to remove after. Because cassava is most commonly grown in other equatorial regions of the world, we have a lot to learn from farmers and chefs in Asia, Africa, and Latin America. Incorporate food forest meals into geography lessons with your children. It's Cuban night! That would be my personal favorite cuisine, but Filipino night and West African night would be lots of fun, too.

My favorite savory cassava recipes are Cuban-style Yuca Con Mojo or Yuca Fries with garlic aioli. For sweeter treats, try Filipino cassava cake or Caribbean cassava pone.

YAMS ARE NOT ORANGE, MY FRIEND, OR FROM A CAN

Dioscorea alata

Marketing works on us in America. We might think that yams are orange and come in cans from the store. This is not so. The kind of yams I am speaking of are commonly grown in Asia and Africa. They've got white flesh or purple flesh and are sometimes called Ube, Winged Yam, or Name (pronounced *nah-may*) Yam. They grow like crazy, one of the most vigorous vines I've ever seen. They are primarily propagated by bulbils, which are seed potatoes that grew on the vines of last year's plant.

One year I had some seed potatoes from HEART village sitting in a cup in my seed cabinet. One day, I opened the cabinet to find two to three foot long vines growing up towards the ceiling. I was astounded. These yam bulbils had no light, no dirt, and no water. That goes to show you how much energy can be stored in roots. Amazing!

When growing, they need a fence, trellis, tree, or something to climb. They grow extremely fast. I've had them climb 30 feet up a tree. Once the rainy season is over and we head into winter, the vines die back to the ground. That's either time to harvest the tuber or leave it in the ground, saving it for next year. If you leave the roots in the ground, they will get larger year after year. There's a YouTube video where Pete Kanaris and his guys found one growing in the wild and hauled it out in a wheelbarrow. It was 157 pounds.[12]

If you have wild areas available for growing, yams is a great choice. It is invasive, but it's invasive food. It's not just birds and butterflies who need to eat, we're part of the ecosystem, too.

Yams are used like potatoes. The white yams are a substitute for white potato, and the purple yams are often used like sweet potato, to make pies, cakes, and other delicious, sweet options.

---

[12] https://www.youtube.com/watch?v=NWPZumb6spo

Good news for you, North Florida! You can grow edible Yamberries, *dioscorea batatas* and *dioscorea japonica*. Sometimes you can find these in international or Asian grocery stores.

TROPICAL TUBERS BEAR GOOD NEWS FOR DIABETICS

There's great news! Both yuca and yams are low glycemic, even more so than sweet potatoes. A normal white potato has a glycemic index of 80 to 90 depending on the preparation method. A sweet potato has a glycemic index of 70, yams of 62, and yuca is only 46! That's about half the sugar of a white potato. I've had clients whose doctors told them they couldn't have white potatoes because they're high in sugar, but they could have yuca. Winning!

SWEET POTATO – EAT THE LEAVES, TOO!

Ipomoea batatas

One of the most important things to note about sweet potatoes is that the leaves are edible. Sweet potato leaves are both delicious and nutritious. The plant has a vining growth habit, and the newest leaves are the best to eat raw. Sweet potato leaves are like spinach, but have a milder, sweeter flavor. I love to sauté the leaves in olive oil or butter. They're high in Vitamin K and have a high nutrient density. Out of dozens of edible greens that grow well in warm climates, sweet potato leaves are one of my favorites!

Sweet Potato tubers need rich soil to do well. Some people grow them in raised beds or grow bags for this reason, but if you're fertilizing your bananas well, then growing them around well mulched banana plants should do just fine. Let them climb and ramble up and around the banana plants. Plant them twelve to eighteen inches apart.

Sweet potatoes like the heat; they grow well planted any time from early spring through the end of June and can be harvested three to four months after planting.

Sweet potatoes are typically started from transplants called "slips." Slips are baby plants that sprout from a mature sweet potato and can be achieved by putting the skinny end of a sweet potato halfway into a glass of water. Slips will grow from the top. You'll want to use slips that are six to nine inches long. If you can acquire cuttings from friends or neighbors who are already growing sweet potatoes that's another way to start new plants. Cuttings will root easily in a glass of water or directly in soil. If working with cuttings, upon planting, try to give young plants some protection from the harsh sun until rooted.

To reduce pest issues and soil depletion, rotate where you plant sweet potatoes at least every two years. Rotating your crops every year is ideal for soil health and better yields.

After harvesting, don't forget to cure your sweet potatoes. I've had clients harvest and eat them right away. They remarked to me, "They tasted like carrots." I was puzzled for a second. Then it dawned on me, and I asked, "Did you cure them?" They said, "No, what's that?" Curing is when you take the newly dug sweet potatoes and leave them in the back of your pantry for at least two weeks. This allows some of the starch to convert to sugar, thus becoming a "sweet" potato. If you don't do this, they taste like carrots, so... cure before consuming. Store cured sweet potatoes in your pantry, not your refrigerator.

MALANGA AND THE FAMILY OF SUPER STARCHY TUBERS

Colocasia esculenta

Malanga, Taro, Eddo, Dasheen, Cocoyam – a lot of names for this awesome family of tubers! Malanga is one of my favorite potatoes and edible greens. It's also a very ornamental plant that looks just like Elephant Ear but is edible. Like cassava, the leaves are only edible cooked. Once the leaves are cooked, the water should be discarded, as the calcium oxalate isn't pleasant to consume. If you're ever eating from the food forest, and something starts tingling on your tongue... stop! This is nature warning you. Boil malanga leaves for 30 minutes, uncovered. Then, dump the water, and add the cooked greens to your recipe.

Malanga should be started in the early spring, as it takes eight to ten months to mature. They can be grown in full sun, part shade, or full shade. I've found that part shade is ideal. These are also great companion plants for bananas, as they should be in rich soil and well-watered. Space them two feet apart.

When harvesting leaves, as with most plants, the newest leaves will be the most tender and delicious once cooked. When it's time to harvest the tubers, just dig up the plant. I usually save the small, side corms (tiny potatoes) for replanting next season.

Malanga roots once harvested can be stored at room temperature for a few weeks, but they'll store in the fridge for longer. Malanga is delicious! It has three times more starch than a white potato, and tastes more like a dumpling. It's an excellent thickener in soups, and I love using it is zuppa toscana.

PERENNIAL BEANS FOR THE WIN!

Cajanus cajan

Most beans are an annual crop. You plant them once, they produce once, and they die. If you're lucky, they'll self-seed, and in the next warm season, you'll have volunteers.

The best perennial bean we grow in the subtropics is pigeon pea, also called *gandules*. It's a short-lived perennial that produces beans annually for 3 to 5 years. You can consume peas or dry beans cooked, green like edamame, or brown, like lentils. The flowers are also edible. Bonus: anything in the legume family also fixes nitrogen in the soil. That means the plants are actively fertilizing the soil, and the leaves of the plant can be used as a chop and drop around your fruit trees. Pigeon pea is daylight sensitive and won't produce flowers and beans until winter. They do best in the warmer parts of Florida.

To start pigeon pea, get some seeds from friends, go to Cody Cove Farm's website for impressive Florida adapted varieties, or roll the dice and go to an international grocery store. Look for them listed as *gandules* or pigeon peas. Soak the beans overnight to speed the germination process. Then, toss them out wherever you'd like to see them grow. I often would toss and then step on them, to make sure they get into the dirt. You could also use a stick to make small indentations in dirt, place a seed in, and then cover it up. They're very forgiving.

The plant grows like a bush or small tree. The best practice to promote wind tolerance is to trim the plant when it's about waist high, forcing it to branch. If you don't do this, pigeon pea tends to grow straight up with only a few branches. Then, when a big wind comes, your tall, straight pigeon pea will fall straight over. If you wonder whether I speak from experience… yes, *I do*. So, learn from my mistakes. If you trim the pigeon pea while young, forcing it to branch, it will become more productive and more resistant to wind. Yay!

Pigeon pea serves so many uses in the food forest. It grows fast and can be used for quick privacy or as a windbreak. It also can be used around plants that are not cold tolerant as an extra layer of protection. Pigeon pea grows quickly and is cheap to acquire.

You can transplant them while young, but do not attempt later. Like many beans, they do not transplant well. It's silly to try. They're cheap and easy to start – if you don't like where it's growing, just cut it down, chop and drop around fruit trees, and start some new pigeon peas where you want them.

PRICKLY PEAR CACTUS: DELICIOUS, NOT A DIVA

Opuntia cacti

I would be remiss if I did not include *nopales*, as it's called in Mexico. This is the easiest-to-grow vegetable that nature ever produced. As a cactus, it's drought tolerant, pest-tolerant and thrives in poor quality sand. That's pretty amazing. Not only that, but the pads are delicious. Many people use them as a substitute for green bell pepper in cooking. They have the flavor of bell pepper with a hint of lemon. If you've eaten out at Mexican restaurants, chances are good that you've had *Nopales* but weren't aware. They're commonly served in fajita bowls. I often use them in eggs, chilis, soups, and nearly any other recipe that calls for a cooked bell pepper. *Nopales* are high in fiber and contain vitamins A, C, calcium, potassium and magnesium.[13]

My prickly pear cactus makes teeny tiny fruits that are nothing to write home about. There's nothing to them. If you're

---

[13]

https://www.urmc.rochester.edu/encyclopedia/content.aspx?ContentTypeID=76&ContentID=11964-1

interested in delicious cactus fruits, you'd be much better off investing in yellow or red dragon fruit.

GREENS FOR POPEYE

We can grow a lot of leafy greens in the food forest. These are not greens you've probably heard of, so it'll require a willingness to learn and experiment. Some are more like kale, collards, spinach, or lettuce, but all are distinct. They've got their own textures and flavors. Give them a try!

Because many of these greens are unfamiliar, I've included flavor profiles and nutritional information.

CHAYA IS THE CHAMP

Cnidoscolus aconitifolius

Nothing packs a protein punch like chaya, also known as Mexican Tree Spinach. Just one serving of chaya has as much protein as an egg, twice the iron of spinach, and more calcium than most vegetables. It is loaded with vitamins, including vitamin A (which is an important nutrient for children especially), vitamin C, folic acid, and vitamin B. Hunger researchers at ECHO Global Farm think chaya holds promise because of the high protein content, and that it could potentially be part of solving malnutrition in subtropical regions. Chaya helps with blood circulation, digestion, and vision. It improves brain function, memory, immunity, and bone health. It reduces inflammation, cholesterol levels, and may help in weight loss. Chaya combats diabetes, arthritis, and renal issues.

Only edible cooked, chaya is a perennial green that will produce edible leaves for many years. Since chaya isn't edible raw, use it as a kale or spinach substitute in cooking – in soups, stews, pasta, etc. Once you've boiled the leaves, the water is perfectly safe to drink and full of Vitamin A. In many cultures, they drink chaya tea for its health benefits.

There are at least two kinds of chaya. There is a deeply lobed variety that is fast-growing, produces a ton of small white blooms, and is excellent for butterflies, specifically attracting monarch and zebra longwings butterflies. Then, there is the maple leaf variety that is best for food. The leaves are more tender, have less pronounced veins, and more vegetative mass per leaf. They are slower growing.

Most chaya looks a little sad in the winter. Sometimes they lose their leaves altogether. Don't worry, that's normal. Spring is coming. The best time to harvest chaya is during the spring and summer when leaves are abundant.

Chaya cannot be cooked or stored in aluminum foil as this can create a toxic reaction. Also, it won't grow north of zone 8. Chaya can handle full sun to partial shade.

Chaya is wildly easy to propagate by stem cutting. Take a cutting of chaya, almost any size will do, from six inches to six feet, and let it sit for two days. You want the end that has been cut to dry out. Then, stick it in soil or sand. I've had chaya root even when I didn't intend for it to. I had cuttings leaned up against the house to plant later. I'm a little ADHD and never got around to planting them. Never fear! They planted themselves, and to my shame, they are growing there, still.

Chaya is a spinach or kale substitute. I've used it in zuppa toscana, chili, marinara sauce, and eggs but one of my favorite ways to use chaya is in ever-so-yummy hot spinach artichoke dip. One time I served this to some vegan friends and their first question was, "is there meat in this?" It sounds crazy, but it's almost like you can taste the protein. You can also serve chaya like collard greens, fried in bacon fat, with garlic and bacon bits thrown in. It's delicious, with a flavor all its own.

KATUK; LEAVES SO SWEET

Breynia androgyna

Katuk is a perennial plant that grows like a shrub and produces an edible leaf crop year-round. It's called sweet leaf in Asia because the leaves have an excellent taste quality, somewhat like a pea, with nutty notes. Young, tender leaves are edible raw or cooked, older leaves would be most suitable cooked. Of all the shrub growth habit greens, it's the easiest to hedge for privacy. It's a shrub that will fill in, get bushy, and colonize an area. It will send up more plants from suckers and seeds.

Katuk's nutritional content is excellent, the leaves contain high protein, fiber, vitamins A, B, and C, potassium, calcium, phosphorus, and magnesium.[14] Katuk is known to increase breastmilk production in lactating mothers.[15]

Katuk is easy to propagate either by cutting or seed. Cuttings are best for those of us who are impatient. Take a ten-to-twelve-inch section of katuk (thicker stem is best) and root in a pot of good dirt in the spring or summer. Keep the pot moist, use mulch on top if you'd like, and keep it in the shade. Once rooted, plant it out in your yard or food forest. Katuk is one of the few greens that prefers part shade to full shade. Give it what it wants!

Katuk is one of my favorite perennial greens. My husband thinks the name sounds funny, like a sideways attempt at sneezing or maybe a curse word, *kaaatuk*! Or, "get your *katuk* over here."

MORINGA; TREE OF LIFE

Moringa oleifera

Moringa is a vigorous, fast-growing, drought tolerant tree useful for food and medicine. Traditionally, the plant is used to cure wounds, pain, ulcers, liver disease, heart disease and cancer. A

---

[14] https://www.eattheweeds.com/edible-katuk-sauropus-androgynus-2/#:~:text=Katuk%E2%80%99s%20nutritional%20content%20is%20outstanding%3A%2049%25%20protein%2C%2018%25,at.55%25%29%3B%20magnesium.55%25%3B%20and%20even%20enough%20iron%20to%20mention.

[15] https://www.semanticscholar.org/paper/The-effect-of-Katuk-leaf-to-breastfeeding-mother%3A-a-Suryawan-Lazarosony/22739b48f7dc62c64b0289d963c8177e43bf9888

poultice made from moringa leaves is a remedy for inflammatory conditions such as glandular inflammation, headache, and bronchitis.[16]

Moringa leaves are edible raw or cooked and are one of nature's most nutritious foods. Leaves have a high content of beta-carotene, minerals, calcium, and potassium. They are an excellent source of protein, vitamin B6, vitamin C, iron, riboflavin, vitamin A, magnesium and antioxidants. The pods are rich in vitamin C. Studies show that moringa may lower blood sugar levels, reduce inflammation, and lower cholesterol. It's medicine.

To demonstrate just how strong the medicinal and nutritional quality is, let's compare moringa to some commonly known foods. Moringa has ten times more vitamins than carrots, seven times more vitamin C than oranges, 15 times more potassium than bananas, and 17 times more calcium than milk.[17] Hence, in some places, it's called the "tree of life" or "miracle tree".

The bark of the tree is useful in the treatment of ulcers, toothache, and hypertension. Roots are found to have a role in the treatment of toothache, helminthiasis, and paralysis. The flowers are used to treat ulcers, enlarged spleen, and to produce aphrodisiac substances. The tree is believed to have powerful

---

[16] https://www.ncbi.nlm.nih.gov/pmc/articles/PMC9916933/

[17] https://www.ncbi.nlm.nih.gov/pmc/articles/PMC8373516/

properties in treating malnutrition in infants and lactating mothers.[18]

I know it's medicine, but people call it the 'horseradish tree' for a reason. The leaves eaten raw have a strong flavor, but when dried and ground into a powder, it's nearly flavorless, which is why people use moringa powder in smoothies, soups, yogurt, etc.

Moringa gets super tall super fast, which is not convenient for harvesting leaves. The only solution is regularly cut the tree back to three feet tall. Baker's Creek sells a dwarf variety of moringa.

Moringa grows best in full sun but can tolerate partial shade. It is drought tolerant but not flood tolerant. Don't plant moringa anywhere that gets too wet for too long.

Moringa seeds are incredible all on their own. Moringa seeds are a source of protein, amino acids, lipids, potassium, phosphorus, sodium, zinc, magnesium, calcium, and vitamin A.[19] Some people remove the outer shell and swallow the seed like they would a vitamin for the medicinal benefits.

What I think is most amazing about moringa seeds is their coagulant and antimicrobial properties that can purify dirty water. I've seen demonstrations at ECHO Global Farm where they put out two glass pitchers of pond water. In one pitcher, they put crushed up moringa seed powder. Within one hour,

---

[18] NIH https://www.ncbi.nlm.nih.gov/pmc/articles/PMC9916933/

[19] https://www.ncbi.nlm.nih.gov/pmc/articles/PMC6593375/

that water is totally clear and 90-99% drinkable.[20] Try it for yourself, go to ECHO Global Farm for a tour, or look it up on YouTube. You'll be amazed! This research has vital significance for parts of the world where access to clean water is a daily struggle.

AIBIKA; EDIBLE LEAF HIBISCUS

Abelmoschus manihot

Edible leaf hibiscus is a perennial vegetable with a shrub-like growth habit that produces highly nutritious greens year-round. The leaves are high in protein, calcium, iron, vitamins A, C, and folic acid.[21] Flowers are also edible and can be used raw or cooked. They've been traditionally used in China to treat chronic kidney disease.[22]

The best ways to eat edible leaf hibiscus are raw or freeze dried. Younger leaves can be used as a lettuce or spinach substitute. Some varieties produce large leaves, and I've used them for lettuce wraps. Older leaves should be cooked due to mucilage. Freeze drying gives them a nice crunch and preserves nutrients.

The crop is easy to grow and requires little care. It does well in Florida's sandy, alkaline soils and makes for an attractive

---

[20] https://allaboutmoringa.info/wp-content/uploads/2020/11/How-to-purify-water-with-moringa-seeds.pdf

[21] https://pfaf.org/native/abelmoschus-manihot/

[22] https://www.ncbi.nlm.nih.gov/pmc/articles/PMC7482509/

specimen in the landscape. In my experience, edible leaf hibiscus prefers to grow in part shade or full shade. Direct sun is too much for this plant, and it withers under the strain of full sun. Additionally, this plant is a short-lived perennial. It will grow for about 18-24 months before starting to decline. Once leaf growth begins to slow and the leaves it produces are significantly smaller, it's time to take cuttings and start new plants. It won't be long before the mother plant is done.

LONGEVITY SPINACH

Gynura procumbens

Safe to eat raw or cooked, longevity spinach boasts many health benefits. It has high levels of antioxidants and nutrients like vitamins A, C, E and K. It has twice the calcium of milk and three times the iron of spinach. It lowers cholesterol and blood pressure; it may help fight cancer, diabetes, and many other ailments.[23] Longevity spinach grows in zones 9-11 and prefers partial shade.

As with most leaf crops, it's the youngest, newest leaves that are the most tender and delicious for eating raw. Select those leaves for your salads, sandwiches, soups, or smoothies. The semi-succulent leaves have a nice crunch with a hint of carrot flavor;

---

[23] https://www.absolutegardener.com/longevity-spinach/

they taste more like cabbage than spinach. Longevity spinach leaves can be freeze dried.

Longevity spinach is extraordinarily useful in the food forest as an edible ground cover. It won't get too tall, but it will sprawl. Use this growth habit to help you cover the ground. Like edible leaf hibiscus, it's a short-lived perennial for zones 9 and warmer. After about 18-24 months, the leaves and stems will start to decline; this is the sign that it's time to take cuttings and make new plants. Longevity Spinach cuttings are easily rooted in soil or a glass of water.

BRAZILIAN SISSOO SPINACH

Alternanthera sissoo

Brazilian sissoo is a lovely, low-growing plant that can do the work of a ground cover in a small space. It grows to be about twelve inches tall and spreads like a mat. There are two varieties, a round leaf variety and a long leaf variety. It's a tropical spinach, so it thrives in a high heat and humid environment. Gratefully, we've got plenty of that! Sissoo is also shade tolerant. It can be eaten raw or cooked and has a very mild flavor. You can propagate it via cuttings, as it roots at the nodes.

OKINAWA SPINACH

Gynura bicolor

Okinawa spinach is an especially attractive herbaceous plant related to longevity spinach. Its leaves are green on top and purple on the bottom. It is considered to be a medicinal vegetable. Leaves can be consumed raw or cooked; any way you enjoy greens. The more you prune this plant, the bushier it will become. Okinawa spinach prefers partial shade and is propagated via cutting.

Okinawa spinach is sometimes called "cholesterol spinach" due to its capacity to help lower cholesterol. The leaves are rich in protein, potassium, fiber, and vitamins C, E, and B group vitamins.[24] Some of the compounds in Okinawa spinach were found to be anti-inflammatory, antioxidant, supportive of healthy blood sugar balance, supportive of liver health, and help skin defend itself from sun damage.[25]

MALABAR SPINACH

Basella alba or Basella rubra

This is a warm weather leaf crop with a vining growth habit. The leaves, shoots, and berries are all edible. The vine will either

---

[24] https://www.sciencedirect.com/science/article/abs/pii/S0963996920302477

[25] https://www.permaculturenews.org/2023/11/03/%E2%80%8B%E2%80%8B%E2%80%8Bokinawa-spinach/

require a trellis or can ramble along the ground. Frequent pruning and harvesting of leaves is good for the plant and will promote a bushier growth habit. Malabar leaves contain calcium, iron, potassium, and vitamins A and C.[26]

There are two varieties of Malabar spinach: green and red. The red variety has ornamental red stems with pink veins on the leaves. It is propagated via seeds and stem cuttings. Malabar leaves are ready to begin harvesting in under two months. The leaves are semi-succulent and have a crunch to them. Malabar spinach makes an excellent addition to soups, stews, and stir-fry.

MOLOKHIA; THE GREENS FROM EGYPT

Corchorus olitorius

Egyptian spinach is an excellent heat-tolerant green for the summer months. The leaves are edible raw or cooked, and best used young. Additionally, toward the end of its growing season, Egyptian spinach produces these small okra-like seed pods that have a delightful crunch to them when eaten out of hand. The flavor reminds me of cucumber. Enjoy them fresh, or let them continue to develop, harden, and dry out if you would like to save the seeds. Other heat-tolerant greens include Lagos spinach and amaranth.

---

[26] https://docs.udc.edu/causes/Fact-Sheet-Malabar-spinach-Basella-alba-is-a-Nutritious-and-Ornamental-Plant.pdf

Egyptian spinach contains fiber, potassium, iron, calcium, magnesium, phosphorous, and selenium, as well as vitamin C, E, K, A, vitamin B6, and niacin. Studies show Egyptian spinach may regulate blood pressure, increase circulation, improve digestion, bone health, heart health, sleep habits and boost the immune system.[27]

---

[27] https://www.organicfacts.net/health-benefits/other/health-benefits-of-molokhia.html

CHAPTER 4
GOING BANANAS FOR BANANAS

I saved the best for last. Bananas are a superior staple crop in many ways. They fruit fast, heavily, year-round in warmer areas and are useful as both a fruit and a vegetable. The drawbacks are that they take up a lot of space and are thus not a great solution for small yards. They can grow very tall... so if you don't want bananas fruiting at 14 feet or higher, be mindful to select dwarf varieties. They also don't tolerate freezing temperatures very well. In colder parts of Florida, I'd recommend a variety called Viente Cohol, which is known for fast ripening. The last thing you want is for a bunch of fruit to emerge right before winter. This variety ripens in only two months instead of the normal four months, potentially saving your harvest.

Bananas have three stages of development, the vegetative stage, the flowering stage, and the fruiting stage. Typically, the first stage takes six months. The last two stages take three to four months each. You could get fruit in the first year.

It's worth mentioning that the stalk which bore fruit, what you might think is a fruit tree, is in fact an herbaceous plant that after it fruits, will die. Cut it down with a machete and chop it up at the base of the pups to feed them. More banana pups, also called suckers, will come up from the ground.

SOURCE BANANAS FOR FREE

Bananas are pretty pricey these days. Depending on your area and the plant size, they can run anywhere from $40 to $80 each. Ouch! Here's the good news. If you pay attention when you drive around, you'll notice neighbors and friends with banana plants. Say please and you might be able to start getting banana pups for free or cheap.

Many people with older banana stands have not managed them well and let them get out of control. Often, they'd be more than happy to let you dig up a few pups. Free labor! Even if they don't want to give them away, perhaps offer $5 or $10 per pup. It's a lot less than you'll pay at a nursery!

PUP SELECTION

There are two kinds of banana pups, called sword suckers and water suckers. Sword suckers are pups with narrow leaves. They're called sword suckers because their young leaves look like swords, long and narrow. This kind of pup is highly preferable as they will make strong bunches with loads of bananas. The other kind of pup has a wide leaf when young and is called a water sucker. They will make pitiful bunches of just a few bananas. Take them if they're all you can get, but if you can select sword suckers, those are ideal. I know many growers who use a machete to cut down water suckers and compost them in place, chop and drop style.

You want to dig banana pups that are two to four feet tall. Smaller ones may not thrive. As you dig out pups, angle your shovel ever-so-slightly towards the mother plant. In the ground is a big white clump of root called the banana corm or mat. Make sure that you get some root on the bottom of your pup, or it may not survive.

RESILIENT IN A FIVE STAR

Strong banana pups with roots are so resilient, you could leave them in a hotel room for a week, and they'd be fine. How do I know, you ask. Have I ever walked through a five-star hotel lobby with a large banana plant on my luggage cart? Why, yes. I have.

Several years ago, I had the opportunity to visit Josh Jamison at Cody Cove Farm just south of Lake Wales. If you're ever in the area, I highly recommend it. Josh offers farm tours on the second and fourth Saturday of every month. While there, he sold me a large pup of SH3640. This amazing banana variety makes large, grocery store-sized bananas, which is rare in the backyard banana world. Almost all commercially available banana varieties produce small bananas. So, this bigger banana variety is coveted.

The banana plant wouldn't fit in my car. It was too tall, so Josh cut the top several feet off with a machete. It was now just the green stalk with roots, no leaves. Josh wrapped the corm in a plastic bag, to protect my van from the dirt on the roots, and I drove off to a fancy hotel in Clearwater Beach where I had to stay for a work gig. At that time, I worked in nonprofit fundraising. So here I am, at the valet of a five-star hotel, putting a five-foot-tall banana plant on my luggage cart with my suitcase and favorite pillow. The bellhop had a few questions, as you might imagine. This is not an ordinary occurrence at the hotel. We got a few quizzical looks from passersby and had a lively conversation on the way to my suite.

The most amazing part of this story is what happened over the next several days. Sitting in a hotel room, deprived of soil, water, and sunlight, the banana plant wrapped in a plastic bag grew! And it didn't just grow a little, it grew a lot. By the end of four days, the leaves had regrown nearly six inches! I was dumbfounded. How amazing! That's the power of energy stored in roots; think of potatoes, which are roots, sprouting in your dark pantry. This is why banana plants can get killed by frost, but if the corm is protected with heavy mulch, they'll come back.

COMPOST PLEASE! FEED YOUR BANANAS AND THEY'LL FEED YOU

Bananas are heavy feeders. What this means to the organic, backyard gardener is that they need as many kitchen scraps, compost, manure, and mulch as you can spare. Now, we have both chickens and pigs, so many of our kitchen scraps go to them. But whatever isn't fed to the farm animals is put on my back porch in a five-gallon bucket. Coffee grinds, eggshells, onion skins, banana peels, citrus rinds. The list goes on. Anything you could throw in compost. I add to this bucket some water, and everything begins to get anaerobic. Be sure to use a bucket with a lid; you're not going to want to smell this! Once it smells like death or feces, good job - it's ready! You can use it like compost tea. Pour the water into watering cans and dilute with water. The ratio doesn't matter much if you're using it on bananas. They could take it straight. On other plants, I might do 30% compost tea to 70% water. Once you've used the water, you'll be left with a delightful sludge. As David the Good says, plants don't have noses, so they won't mind. I would use a few cups of sludge per plant, then add some mulch on top to keep racoons and other pests away.

If you can get your hands on manure, that's garden gold. Bananas would be happy with manure almost any way you can get them. The only exception is newly planted bananas. Baby banana plants can't handle fresh manure, it's too hot and will burn the plant. Aged manure would be fine for young plants. And mulch will make them happy-happy. Think Phil Robertson, saying "happy-happy" in his Cajun twang. Just in case you thought that was a typo, it wasn't.

Bananas would be happy in a rainforest and thus they need tons of water. The average rainfall in Florida is not adequate. Planting them near lakes, ponds, or wet areas is a good idea. To clarify, by wet areas, I don't mean areas that flood for more than a day or two. If planting bananas next to a lake or pond, plant them near the high-water line. If bananas are subjected to more than a few days of flooding the roots will start to rot. The best solution for most homeowners is to plant bananas where you could easily run a drip line or soaker hose. For most, this means planting bananas near a hose nozzle, putting a two-way splitter on it (so you can run a drip line in one direction and a hose the other way), and running a soaker hose through a clump of your bananas. Many drip lines are 30, 50 or 100 feet long. This is the best way to ensure that your bananas are getting slowly and constantly watered. Watch the plants explode with growth, producing bunches of fruit, and lots of new pups. You can thank me later.

TO BANANA CIRCLE OR NOT TO BANANA CIRCLE

There's this concept in food forest world called a banana circle. Early in my journey, I was a fan of this, planting bananas in circles and digging out the center, filling it with compost and other organic materials to feed the bananas. This seemed like a genius idea. Unfortunately, time has proven that this was not advisable. Typically, bananas are planted two to three feet apart in a banana circle, which is way too close. Once the mother plant dies, more pups come, the mat spreads and they need more space. They spread every year. Recently I've had to dig banana plants out of my banana circles and move them to prevent crowding. I'm now planting bananas six to eight feet apart.

HOW MANY BANANAS?

How much does your family enjoy bananas? Let's think through a calendar year. How often could your family consume a forty-pound bunch of bananas? I have three growing boys who love bananas – bananas fresh, bananas in smoothies, and bananas can even be used green as a vegetable, like a potato. My family could consume a bunch at least every other week. There are 52 weeks in a year, so 26 banana plants wouldn't be a bad idea for us. But that may not fit in your average suburban yard. What if you'd like a bunch a month? You would need 12 plants. Or, every other month, you'd need six plants. In warmer climates, bananas fruit nearly year-round, so if you have an abundance of them, they're always producing.

BANANA STAND MAINTENANCE

Ideally, I don't allow more than four to five pups per banana plant, maximum. You want the mother plant to focus on making fruit, not pups. If your plant is producing a lot of pups, dig one out now and then. Sometimes I remove a pup based on the direction it's growing --- it's growing into another banana plant, it's getting too close to a sidewalk or other structure, or it's growing at a 45-degree angle. Growing at too severe an angle will be a problem when it comes time to fruit, and the plant is struggling to stay upright under the strain of a 40-pound bunch of bananas.

BLOWING OVER

Bananas are shallow-rooted and are thus susceptible to wind damage. Solutions are to plant near windbreaks, like buildings, fences, or hedges. Of course, plant a few feet away because they'll spread. Another solution is to plant other plants near the bananas that could serve as a windbreak. Pigeon pea or Mexican sunflower would be a good choice because they're fast growing and useful for chop and drop. If you happen to have bamboo on the property, they're my favorite windbreak.

When a big hurricane is coming, and you have beautiful banana plants loaded with fruit, so they're already nearly falling over, you have a problem. Gratefully, the solution is simple. Take two bamboo or areca poles that are about as tall as your banana plant. Lash them together with rope or strong twine. Once tied together, cross them into an X. Put the base of the X up under the banana plant to support it. This is your best chance to withstand hurricane force winds, prevent it from falling over, and keep fruit ripening on the plant.

CHAPTER 5
LET'S GET FRUITY

First, the bad news. In warmer parts of Florida, we can't grow stone fruits. Most kinds of apples and pears seen in the grocery store are out of the question. But there's good news! We can grow a ton of delicious, prolific, tropical fruits. Some you've had before like mango and avocado, and others you may not have heard of, like jujube and longan. If you're willing to learn, we live in an area where there are lots of interesting fruits that are worth trying!

Besides banana and papaya, which are quick, prolific producers, my favorite fruit trees are as follows: sapodilla, starfruit, jackfruit, mango, avocado, jujube, and mulberry. There are others, like mamey sapote, longan, and dragon fruit, that deserve an honorable mention. Lychee is intentionally left off my list. There's a new disease emerging, called lychee mites, that has the potential to completely wipe out lychee in Florida within the next decade. The cousin of lychee, longan, is more reliable. It bears young, fruits more readily, and doesn't have major disease issues. If you enjoy lychee, opt for longan instead.

North Florida can grow stone fruits! If you want to try to grow tropicals, grab yourself a copy of David the Good's book, *Push the Zone*. He spent years building food forests in North Florida. Some of the best fruit trees for North Florida include but are not limited to, apples, pomegranates, figs, loquats, peaches, pears, plums, persimmons, kiwis, mulberries, and pawpaws. No one up there is going to starve. There's lots to choose from!

CONTINUOUS HARVESTS

If the goal is food production, then one of the answers must be planting fruit trees that bear fruit multiple times per year. This makes a massive difference in the amount of food produced. For example, mango and avocado both fruit once annually. At maturity, these trees can produce 200 pounds of fruit on average. Sapodilla and starfruit both fruit several times during the year, almost continually, and at maturity produce 400 to 500 pounds of fruit annually. This is the power of more than one season.

SWEET STARFRUIT

Carambola, commonly called starfruit, can be grown in zones 9-11. I give this disclaimer: if as a child in the 80's or 90's you ate starfruit and you didn't love it, give it another chance. Many of the starfruit varieties we're planting today weren't available then.

The new varieties originated in Asia and have such sweet fruit! This is *not* your grandma's starfruit, so if you didn't care for it before, give it another go.

Starfruit is sweet and juicy! I love eating them fresh, but you can also slice them thin and put them in salads, freeze them for smoothies, use them fresh in salsas and chutneys, put them on the grill, add to stir fry, use as a garnish, dehydrate them, or use in juices, jams, or desserts. That's a lot of versatility!

Starfruit is high in fiber, vitamin C, and antioxidants. People with kidney disease should not consume starfruit.[28] One tree can produce so much fruit that you may not be able to use it all yourself. If you have an abundance of starfruit, there are lots of options. Give your children a chance at entrepreneurship and sell them! Why not let your yard pay you back? Or if you're a generous soul, simply share them with neighbors and friends. Or trade fruit for plants! If you're like me and you've got livestock, use any starfruit that got bruised or fell to the ground to feed pigs. Give to chickens as an occasional treat. Your animals will be happier and healthier for it.

Starfruit trees tend to bear fruit young. I don't allow that. When it's newly planted the best thing for it to put energy into is developing a strong root system. It's not going to do that if it's putting all its energy into fruit. So, pick off young fruits. This

---

[28] https://www.kidney.org/atoz/content/why-you-should-avoid-eating-starfruit

encourages the tree to root and establish a sturdy trunk with good branching that promotes airflow.

Starfruit trees benefit from some wind protection. I tend to plant them near hedges, houses, and other mature trees. They don't get more than 20 or 30 feet tall if left unpruned, making them much smaller than mango, jackfruit, and sapodilla. That said, starfruit can tolerate some shade. They still need about 6-8 hours of sun to be at peak production. You also want to prune off any low-hanging branches that will drag on the ground when loaded down with heavy fruit.

Some of my favorite starfruit varieties are 'Fwang Tung' and 'Kari'. Other good ones include 'Sri Kembangan' and 'Arkin'. In areas that are prone to frost, young starfruit trees need protection. If the temperature is going to get below freezing, cover young trees in a sheet or blanket. Deep water the root system before the cold moves in. Mulch the ground and pray for the best.

STATELY SAPODILLA

Manilkara zapota

Sapodilla is one of my favorite fruit trees for a few reasons, its ornamental value, delectable flavor, and how prolific they are. Sapodillas are among the prettiest fruit trees. At my local botanical garden, Mounts, they planted sapodillas in the parking lot; to the untrained eye, they look like magnolia trees. They're both evergreen trees that keep their leaves year-round. They have large, glossy leaves and a nicely rounded shape. I recommend sapodilla for planting in front yards, particularly when cosmetic concerns are a consideration. Of the fruit trees I routinely put in food forest designs, sapodilla is one of the most handsome tree specimens. Luckily, sapodilla is also wind tolerant and drought tolerant. I *love* trees that aren't divas.

The fruit of sapodilla is outstanding. It's soft and sweet with a complex flavor profile, sometimes called the "brown sugar fruit". Imagine biting into a soft pear soaked in brown sugar and cinnamon. A sapodilla tastes like that. It's phenomenal! I love to eat it out of hand. There's one variety called 'Butterscotch' due to its candy-like flavor. Other varieties I commonly plant include 'Alano', 'Molix', 'Morena', and 'Hasya'.

Sapodilla is truly a tropical tree. A mature tree can handle temperatures above 26 degrees. A freeze in 1989 killed and severely damaged many mature trees in Stuart, where the temperature dropped to 26 for two nights in a row.

ALL-PURPOSE PAPAYA

Carica papaya

Papaya is one of the most important plants to include in your food forest for a variety of reasons. It grows fast and can produce fruit within nine months. As far as fruit trees are concerned, it's one of the most economical to acquire. It also takes up a lot less space than most fruit trees. In a space of five feet by five feet, you have a fast-growing plant that was cheap, taking up little room, making 50 to 100 pounds of fruit in the first year. Crazy! That said, papaya is a short-lived perennial. It'll make fruit annually for about two to four years, then decline. This is why I recommend planting at least one papaya every year, so you have plants at various stages of maturity.

Papaya is one of the most versatile crops grown in the subtropics. You can use the fruit green like a vegetable or you can wait until it ripens and becomes sweet. The biggest mistake I see Americans make is waiting too long, until the fruit is totally yellow or orange. By then, the fruit is rotten. You want to pick papaya off the tree when it's starting to turn from green to yellow, and then give it a few days on the counter to ripen. Even ripe papaya can have a weird smell, like stinky socks. A squeeze of lime juice remedies this. We love freezing papaya and using it in smoothies. It's the perfect texture for tropical fruit smoothies!

Ripe papaya is rich in vitamin C, vitamin A, folate, and potassium. Early research suggests that the antioxidants in papaya may slow the progression of cancer, reduce inflammation, reduce the risk of heart disease, and keep your skin looking youthful.[29] There is an emerging body of research on the medicinal potential of consuming papaya seeds in small quantities. The seeds are anti-bacterial, anti-inflammatory, anti-

[29] https://www.healthline.com/nutrition/8-proven-papaya-benefits#TOC_TITLE_HDR_4

diabetic, anti-obesity, anti-parasitic and are wound healing agents.[30] The seeds are spicy, tasting like black pepper mixed wasabi.

I enjoy green papaya in a variety of ways. I make a Thai green papaya salad, which is shredded green papaya, shredded carrot, and an Asian ginger dressing. Easy peasy. Top with roasted peanuts or a protein if you'd like. It's delicious! My dinner guests go back for seconds. Another way to use green papaya is to add it to soups as a vegetable. I also enjoy it pickled in vinegar and sugar with carrots, chayote, and red pepper. This is commonly enjoyed in the Philippines and referred to as "Atchara" if you're looking for recipes online. Pickled papaya is the perfect tangy side dish. Just the mention of it makes my mouth water. Lastly, there is some research showing that fermented green papaya is not only good for your gut, but it can also help people struggling with anemia, cancer, and Alzheimer's.[31] Note of caution for pregnant mamas: pregnant women should not eat green papaya, as unripe papaya contains papain and latex, which can trigger contractions and early labor.[32]

There is an annoying pest that can foil your best laid plans for an abundant papaya harvest. It's the papaya fruit fly, commonly

---

[30] https://www.researchgate.net/publication/358964030_Papaya_Seeds_Treasure_of_Nutrients_and_a_Promising_Preservative

[31] https://www.ncbi.nlm.nih.gov/pmc/articles/PMC8870802/

[32] https://www.healthline.com/health/papaya-in-pregnancy

mistaken as a wasp due to its long abdomen and yellow and black coloring. What happens is that you notice a hole towards the top of your papaya, or some droppings on it. Some papaya might be okay, but others, you'll cut open and find the ripe fruit full of fly larva that look like maggots. Gross! There are a few ways to protect against this fruit fly. One way is to use mesh organza bags. Buy the larger 8x12 inch bags based on the size fruit you expect. I cover the fruit with a bag when young, so the fly can't get in. You could also spray the area with Neem oil. One other thing to do is kill the fly, if you see him! Lastly, don't leave rotten fruit lying on the ground as the fly will lay eggs in it. Be sure to throw away any infested fruit and keep that area clear of any past ripe papaya.

The versatility of papaya is incredible. You've got loads of vegetables, fruit, and if all else fails, food for your animals. With most papaya plants costing about $20 to $40, that's unbeatable for the price tag.

JUICY JACKFRUIT

Artocarpus heterophyllus

Like sapodilla, jackfruit is also a handsome tree specimen, with large, glossy leaves and a nice canopy shape. Jackfruit has an upright, somewhat compact growth habit. What's great about this is that when working with small yards, you can plant jackfruit about ten feet away from other trees and structures because unlike many fruit trees it does not have a sprawling growth habit. A mature jackfruit can produce a lot of food in a small space.

Jackfruit is one of the fastest growing fruit trees in the subtropics and one of the only trees that grows true to seed. Grafting isn't required. The jackfruit is the largest fruit in the world that's produced on trees, weighing up to 80 pounds. The spiky fruit is interesting and beautiful to look at. As the fruit ripens, it puts off a sweet aroma.

Both the seeds and fruit are edible. The fruit I've had tasted like Juicy Fruit gum or Tutti Fruity candy – a mix of all kinds of tropical flavors. Some varieties of jackfruit had stronger hints of citrus, pineapple, or mango, but all were delicious. If you aren't using the seeds to grow more jackfruit trees, then cook them. The seeds are useful like potatoes and can be made into hummus.

Similar to sapodilla, if ornamental value is a concern, jackfruit can make an excellent choice for front yards.

It's worth noting that jackfruit produce both male and female flowers, and the male flowers look a lot like fruit. Male flowers are typically smaller and lack a swollen, thick base where it connects to the tree. The flowers that look like young fruit produce pollen, die, and fall off the tree. People are often confused by this and wonder "Why do all the little fruits on my jackfruit turn black and die?" Those were male flowers, useful for pollination. Female flowers are larger and have a thick stalk connecting them to the tree. These flowers may develop into fruit when pollinated. Jackfruit typically does not require hand pollination.

Young jackfruit trees are susceptible to critters nibbling on bark. If they eat all the way around the base of the tree, that's called girdling, and could eventually kill the tree. To prevent this, use a tree protector or plastic spiral guard. It's more of a problem with young trees that have tender, tasty bark. Older trees don't tend to have this challenge. And for some reason, my wild bunnies prefer jackfruit bark more than others.

MAGNIFICENT MANGO

Mangifera indica

One of the best tropical fruits to grow is everyone's favorite: mango. Sweet and juicy when ripe, mango is a delicious treat. We love to eat mango dried, fresh, or frozen in smoothies. There are almost limitless ways to use this delicious tropical fruit. Mango has vitamin C, potassium, folate, and fiber. It can lower the risk of cardiac disease and stroke.

Mango trees are drought tolerant. At maturity, a mango tree can produce 100 to 300 pounds of fruit.

We can select mango cultivars that fruit at different times. There are hundreds of mango varieties available in the commercial nursery trade. Variety selection can be a little daunting. Early season mangoes fruit in April and May, mid season mangoes fruit in June and July, while late season mangoes fruit into August and September.

My top recommended varieties are:

Early season varieties –
'Carrie'
'Angie'
'Rosiegold'

Mid season varieties –
'Orange Sherbet'
'Pickering'
'Bailey's Marvel'
'Pineapple Pleasure'

Late season varieties –
'Venus'
'All Summer'
'Beverly'
'Candy Corn'
'Kent'

If you can get it, there's a variety called 'Choc-Anon' which can fruit twice a year, in the winter from November to January, and sometimes in July as well. For this reason, some call it the "miracle mango". This mango variety list is extremely subjective. Ask anyone who loves mangoes, and they might give you a completely different list. This list is based on mangoes I've tried, folks I've talked to, and varieties that are commonly available in my region.

Dwarf mangoes are an excellent choice for people with small yards, HOA's, and anyone who doesn't want to have to do lots of pruning with a hand saw as the tree gets older.

For dwarf and semi-dwarf variety mangoes, select:

Early season varieties –

'Angie'

'Carrie'

'Dwarf Hawaiian'

'Glenn'

Mid season varieties –

'Cogshall'

'Fairchild'

'Honey Kiss'

'Ice Cream'

'Julie'

'Nam Doc Mai'

'Pickering'

Late season varieties –

'Keitt'

'Lil Gem'

POISON IVY BITES. MANGO CAN, TOO.

I know that sounds scary. Don't panic. Just be aware that the sap and skin of mango contains urushiol, the same oil found in poison ivy and poison oak.[33] People who haven't had much exposure to poison ivy are less likely to develop a sensitivity to mango skin and sap. You could read the scientific literature on this, but here's my best advice. When cutting mangoes, wear latex gloves. If you get exposed to poison ivy or mango sap, do not attempt to wash it off with water; it won't work. That's now how to remove plant oil from skin. Instead, use Tecnu scrub, Zanfel, or another poison ivy wash. Keep this on hand. If you don't have one of these, scrub vigorously with a ribbed towel. The key is friction. Another idea would be to use Gojo (that's how mechanics get grease off their hands) or any soap with grit. Learn to identify poison ivy and teach your children to do the same. An ounce of prevention is worth a pound of cure.

MANGO SHAPE AND TIPPING

Fruit trees should be shaped like lollipops, with branching starting at three to five feet. I've seen mango trees where the

---

[33] https://www.ncbi.nlm.nih.gov/pmc/articles/PMC6861053/

branching starts at 10 or 12 feet high. That isn't ideal. If I had a tree like that, I would take a hand saw and cut the tree back to three or four feet, to force it to branch lower and develop a nice shape for easy harvesting. Never fear, you're not going to kill the tree. In mango groves across India, they routinely cut old trees down to three feet. We're talking about trees that are 30 or 40 feet tall. Consider this, if the tree is 40 feet tall, the roots are 40 feet deep. You can't kill the tree by cutting it low, you'll just get a lower, more compact tree with better shaping. Drastic pruning like that will mean you sacrifice a season or two of fruit. But it'll be worth it in the long run.

Always use clean tools when pruning fruit trees, especially if you cut into a diseased tree. You can spread disease between trees by pruning with dirty tools.

If buying a mango tree at a nursery, look for a nice tree shape and branching that starts low. As a young mango tree grows, proper pruning when young will ensure more vigorous fruiting. This is called mango tipping. Dr. Richard Campbell has some videos on YouTube showing how it's done.

APPETIZING AVOCADO

Persea americana

A classic fruit in the subtropics is avocado. Personally, it's one of my favorite fruits to eat. In South Florida, we have varieties that fruit as early as May and as late as February. So, for my food forest clients who really enjoy avocado, I recommend planting as few as three trees or as many as five or six. If you're selective, getting cultivars that fruit every other month, you could have a schedule that looks like this, an avocado producing for you in May, July, September, November, and February. That's pretty cool, right? Rather than just having one to two months of avocado production, you have ten months of avocado production. Through wise variety selection, you expand the season.

Early season varieties –

Donnie (May-June)

Simmonds (June-July)

Mid season varieties –

Catalina (July-Sept)

Day (July-Sept)

Brogdon (July-Sept)

Late season varieties –

Winter Mexican (Oct-Nov)

Choquette (Oct-Feb)

Maria Black (Nov-Jan)

Monroe (Nov-Jan)

Oro Negro (Nov-Jan)

Hall (Nov-Feb)

WET FEET ARE A KILLER

Avocado is the one variety of fruit tree that is extremely unforgiving when it comes to flooding. They cannot take 'wet feet'. If your property floods, find high ground or plant them on mounds. I've heard many a tale, 'we planted an avocado, but it died' and when I ask about standing water duration and flooding, that's almost always the culprit.

If you're in zone 7 you'll need to grow avocados in a greenhouse. But zone 8 has some hope with these cold hardy varieties: Mexicola, Bacon, Brogdon, Del Rio (Pryor), Fuerte, May, Opal (Lila), Wilma (Brazos Belle), and Winter Mexican. These trees are cold hardy when they're fully mature. Young trees will need protection from cold snaps. A light blanket can help, as well as putting a heat source under the blanket, like Christmas lights or a camping lantern. Be sure not to use LED lights as they don't emit heat. Some food forest enthusiasts in colder parts of Florida use burn barrels.

BURN BARRELS: WE DID START THE FIRE

"We didn't start the fire. It was always burning since the world's been turning." Sorry if I've got Billy Joel lyrics stuck in your head now. I couldn't help myself.

Burn barrels aren't for the faint of heart. They're for brave folks with a bit of space trying to grow tropical fruit trees in places where that's tough. Here's how it works: you'd plant your tropical fruit trees in a circle. Then, on very cold nights, you'd start a fire in a 55-gallon metal barrel in the center of the circle. Josh Jamison of Cody Cove Farm recorded that it can raise the temperature three to four degrees up to 60 feet away. It's worth noting that this is not legal in some municipalities, so let's hope your neighbors like you. Give them some fruit!

Planting tropical fruit trees near areas with windbreaks is another idea to protect them from cold temperatures. Consider planting them near a hedge, not too far from a house, fence, or other natural barrier. If planting windbreaks to protect fruit trees I'd strongly consider clumping bamboo. Other food forest plants you could use to create windbreaks around the fruit trees are pigeon pea, chaya, katuk, Mexican sunflower, lemongrass, or vetiver grass.

MERRY MULBERRY

Morus spp.

Mulberry is legitimately one of my most favorite food forest fruits. It fruits quickly, in the first year, and is prolific, fruiting multiple times per year with pruning. You can easily grow more trees from cuttings. It produces leaves that are both edible and medicinal. Mulberry trees are drought tolerant; they aren't divas. Mulberry is an all-around winner in my opinion.

There are lots of varieties of mulberry. Some are winners. Some are losers. Here's my experience.

I love Dwarf Thai, World's Best, and Illinois Everbearing. They all make a ton of fruit and are a larger berry. I've heard good things about Shangri-La. I've personally found Pakistan, Green Mulberry, and Everbearing to be overrated. My Pakistan Mulberry might be fighting nematodes, best case scenario, but it's producing very little and I'm threatening to cut it down. My Green Mulberries always got stolen by squirrels and birds, so I cut it down last year. I'm pretty ruthless. Produce or die! Everbearing Mulberry makes the tiniest mulberries in the history of mulberries, and the name, Everbearing, is a total marketing gimmick. All mulberries are everbearing. So, why would you want the tiniest fruit when larger fruiting varieties are available?

I only plant mulberries with a dwarf growth habit. One way to tell whether a plant is dwarf is leaf size. If the leaves are the size of your hand, that's good. They won't get to 50 feet tall. If the leaves are the size of your face, stay away. Unless you want mulberries to feed the birds. I don't know about you, but I can't collect mulberries at 50 feet up in the air.

Propagating mulberry can be tricky at first. I've found that shorter size cuttings do better than longer. You want hardwood cuttings that are about six to eight inches long. Root them in soil in the shade, watering often. After a few weeks, you should see new leaves emerging from the nodes. Once the plant is established, feel free to plant it out in your food forest in a full sun location.

Mulberry trees are deciduous, meaning they lose their leaves during the winter. Sometimes in the fall the leaves start to turn yellow or brown or get eaten by bugs. Never fear, this is the normal seasonal cycle. Come spring, your mulberry will be flush with berries and new growth!

A note on the leaves: it is the mulberry tips that are edible, the new growth, that's still light green and can easily bend. That tender new growth is delicious. I enjoy it in soup or stir fry. There is one variety called Edible Leaf Mulberry that's cultivated entirely for the leaves. There are supplements made from Mulberry leaves, and some folks dry the leaves to use in tea.

Mulberry leaves are highly nutritious, and loaded with flavonoids and antioxidants. For centuries mulberry leaves have been used in traditional Chinese medicine for their healing properties, some of which have been proven by scientific study. Mulberry leaves are anti-inflammatory, can help lower blood sugar, promote heart health, and are effective against obesity, diabetes, fibrosis, and arthritis.[34]

The only thing that holds up some people is the tree's nematode susceptibility. If you've had mulberry trees die, try a nematode-resistant variety like Illinois Everbearing.

Once you've got trees loaded with ripe mulberries, you have a lot of options. Eat them out of hand; this is my favorite way to enjoy

---

[34] https://www.organicfacts.net/mulberry-tree-leaf.html

mulberry. Freeze them for smoothies. Make jam, jelly, or pie. You can substitute mulberry for raspberry or blackberry in most recipes. I find mulberry to be much sweeter than blackberry. It's the easiest berry to grow in Florida, bar none.

JAZZY JUJUBE

Ziziphus jujuba

Sometimes you don't know how amazing a rare fruit is until you taste it. So it was for me with Jujube. One of the challenges with rare fruit is you can't just waltz into the grocery store and find it. You need to know someone who has the tree, and then go see them precisely when the fruit is in season. I tasted my first ripe jujube last year, and I was in love. I immediately bought a jujube tree for myself and began recommending it to all my clients. For parts of the state where we can't grow apples, jujube is a great alternative. It's the size of a plum, tastes like a cross between an apple and pear, with a delightful crunch and sweet notes. My young sons also enjoyed the fruit, and the tree produced quite a lot!

Jujube trees have a weeping growth habit, normally stay about 15-20 feet tall, and bear fruit young. The trees prefer a full sun location. They are cold tolerant, drought tolerant, and require little maintenance. Three criteria that make jujube decidedly not a diva. You can enjoy the fruit fresh, dried, boiled, stewed or baked. Where it was originally cultivated in China, many enjoy it dried. It's for this reason that the jujube is also known as the Chinese Date.

CITRUS: A LOST CAUSE?

Citrus tends to get sick in Florida. Just drive through the orange groves and tell me if the trees look healthy. They're mostly either half-dead or covered in white bags. Those are Tree Defender bags that protect young trees from the greening disease that has decimated the citrus industry in Florida. Because citrus tend to struggle, I don't recommend planting them, or only plant varieties that are known to be greening tolerant.

Developed by the University of Florida, Sugar Belle is a hybrid mandarin that can survive the greening disease and is cold tolerant, surviving temperatures as low as 18 degrees. This fruit ripens from November to December, and like all citrus, it's showy. I love seeing lovely orange fruits hanging in the green leaves! Other greening tolerant varieties include "Tango", "Bingo", "13-51", and "Sundragon", a new USDA release. Many lemon varieties also seem to be somewhat tolerant. Try "Improved Meyer", "Eureka" or "Ponderosa".

FRUIT TREE BUYING GUIDE

Make sure you buy trees from a nursery who have expertise in which fruit tree varieties and cultivars perform well in your region. If you want help learning the best ones, an excellent resource is *Florida's Best Fruiting Plants* by Charles Boning. It's like the Bible of fruit trees in Florida. My mentor Heather Dorsey taught me a long time ago that you don't just want a mango or a longan, you want to walk into the nursery knowing exactly which variety you'd like, as well. For most fruit trees, you want a grafted variety. The nursery staff should be knowledgeable and helpful, or you should find another nursery. Nurseries that specialize in rare fruit trees are gems.

Look at the thickness of the tree's trunk. If you're buying in a particular size, you want to select the thickest trunk as that's an indication of age. Make sure there aren't cracks or wounds on the trunk. Check the health of the leaves. They should be vibrant, green, and free from spots or signs of disease. Next, look at the branching and shaping, especially if you're buying a large tree. Has this tree been properly pruned?

HOW TO PLANT A FRUIT TREE

The most important part of the process is planting your fruit tree, and sadly it's easy to make mistakes that hinder the long-term growth of your tree. How do I know? Failure is success if you learn from it!

When we first moved to Jupiter Farms, I knew I wanted a food forest. I had started growing raised bed gardens and fruit trees at my little house in the city, but we went from having a quarter acre to having more than two acres. That was pretty exciting! At the time, I had a new baby, so, I hired a landscaper to plant the 30+ fruit trees I had purchased from a rare fruit tree nursery.

This landscaper marketed himself as a food forest guy, and while he loved the concept, he made some mistakes that seriously hindered the growth of the trees. Many had to be dug up years later because they never rooted.

What was his big error you ask? It's a common one: putting compost in the planting hole. Lots and lots of well-intentioned people do this, and I understand the logic. We think it'll help the tree. Bad news; it won't.

You don't want the tree's roots to be content right where it was planted. You want the roots to run hard and fast into native soil, looking for nutrients. Your fruit tree's roots have no incentive to go looking for the good stuff if you put it all in the hole. They'll just sit there, and it'll stunt their growth. Deep roots are a high priority. Too much nutrition in the hole slows the tree's development.

What's the solution? Put all your compost and soil amendments on top, like a top dressing after planting; earthworm castings, azomite, and biochar are all good choices in addition to aged compost. Don't use fresh manure or anything that will burn the plants. As always, your final top dressing is dye-free mulch or oak leaves.

WATER IN THE HOLE!

Another critical element to planting is irrigating the hole while you fill it in with dirt. This is to prevent the formation of air pockets underneath the root ball. If you get air pockets, the tree will never grow. In addition to other issues, I believe this also happened to some of the fruit trees that had to be dug up years later. Roots don't grow through air pockets, so be diligent to use water while planting as this can help soil backfill the areas where it's supposed to be.

PLANT HIGH

Most fruit trees should be planted high. Over time, the tree may settle and sink into the ground. If that happens, you want the tree settling down to ground level. If it settles beneath ground level, that means heavy rains may leave the trunk sitting in water, which will kill some fruit trees, especially avocado. For this reason, I recommend planting fruit trees about two to three inches above ground level. Plant avocado trees three to four inches high.

The only exceptions to this are banana and papaya. Papaya can be planted at ground level. Banana might benefit from having a shallow 3-6 inch hole dug, and be planted with a small moat around it. You want the area around the banana to hold water.

DID IT DIE?

If you think your fruit tree died, don't dig it up quite yet. Do the scratch test. Using your fingernail or a knife, scratch off the bark or outer layer of skin on the trunk. If it's green underneath, good news! Your tree is alive! It might just be dormant if deciduous.

Several years ago, I transplanted a longan tree two or three times… this is not advisable. The tree had looked dead for a month or two, so one day I finally gave up hope and went out to dig it up. Right before I put the shovel in the ground, I saw a tiny bud forming! It's alive! Today, that longan tree is twelve feet tall, twelve feet wide, and fruiting. So, never give up! Unless you've done the scratch test, and it is brown underneath. Then, you give up. But don't forget to scratch lower down on the trunk. Sometimes, a tree is dead up near the top but still alive down near the root ball. I've killed more trees than I can count, for a variety of reasons. Winston Churchill once said, "Success is stumbling from failure to failure without any loss in enthusiasm." You could say I've been *successful*.

FINDING COMMUNITY

This might be my favorite aspect of food forest: sharing the love. If you go on Facebook or Nextdoor, chances are good that there other people in your town or nearby who are building food forests. Typically, they've got plants you don't have, and you have plants they don't have. Many plants can grow from cuttings. Make a list of the plants you have, both edible and ornamental, that can be easily propagated. Keep that list handy, so you can offer to trade for the things you want.

If you don't know what plants in your yard can be propagated by cutting, turn to Google. Once I figured out what a plant was, I'd just Google the name of the plant and the word 'propagate' or 'propagate by cutting'. You figured out pretty quickly which plants could be grown easily from cuttings.

Part of my journey into starting Food Forest DIY as a consulting business included offering food forest tours. I was so excited about the food forest that I posted on Facebook and Nextdoor offering tours on a certain Saturday morning for anyone interested. At that time, it was just a hobby, and I didn't charge. Every time I offered a tour there'd be a dozen or more people who'd show up. People were hungry to learn, and I was thrilled to teach. I gave away hundreds of cuttings and seeds, and years later, it was gratifying to see the trees in neighbor's yards that had grown from my generosity. I was ready to share with others, and they shared with me. Go, and do likewise.

Here's my original list of things I had to share with others, by either cutting or seed.

Plants to Trade:
- Cassava/Yuca
- Chaya/Mexican Spinach Tree
- Longevity Spinach
- Cranberry Hibiscus
- Edible Leaf Hibiscus
- Dwarf Thai Mulberry
- Red Mombin/Hog Plum
- Katuk

- Prickly Pear Cactus
- Dragon fruit
- Aloe
- Firebush
- Knock Out Roses
- Mexican Sunflower
- Seeds – Egyptian Spinach, Okra, Yardlong Beans, Pigeon Pea, Broccolini

MAKE A LIST OF WHAT YOU'VE GOT!

I reached out to neighbors on Facebook who were creating food forests and sent them my list. I invited them over to see my place, and I went over to see theirs. Within a short span of time, I built a community of people who were interested in growing food, preserving food, and making medicine. Everyone has their gifts and specialties. Some are great at grafting, seed saving, or curating impressive recipes. Everyone plays a part. This is the kind of community that's resilient! We want to foster this and help it grow. Host potlucks, food forest tours, medicinal meetups, and plant swaps. Do what you can to network with like-minded people who live nearby and encourage each person in what they're good at.

A note about fear: some people are building food forests because they're concerned about the times we live in. They see the signs of decline and want food security for their family. I understand.

But sometimes, this concern grows into fear and leads people to keep their food forests hidden. They don't want neighbors to know that they're growing food. I understand the instinct for self-preservation, but I'd like to counter this with an idea. What if, rather than hiding and trying to protect what we have, we openly tried to inspire others. I've never hidden my food forest. Everyone knows I'm growing food, and my neighbors view me as a community resource, an important source of knowledge and information. In the first eighteen months in business, my company installed 40+ food forests and inspired hundreds more. We planted hundreds of fruit trees and thousands of plants. We educated and encouraged people to keep growing food at home. My neighborhood is now much more resilient, in part, because of my influence and the fact that I didn't cave to fear. I didn't hide. We need to build strong, resilient communities filled with like-minded people who are committed to one another.

That's not to say that I trust everyone. I don't. I believe God gave me the gift of discernment; an ability to know who carries light and who carries darkness. Most people have a bit of both. Some think they carry light, but the fruit of their life is darkness. It's subtle but easy to spot if you have eyes to see. There are neighbors who I visited once and won't visit again. Trust your gut. It's good to know your immediate neighbors, to be sure. You need to know who is trustworthy, and who is not. And, I'm just going to say it: an armed society is a polite society. Any good mama bear will both feed and protect her young.

ANIMALS COMPLETE THE SYSTEM

You may be figuring out by now that this food forest of yours can grow a lot of food, and create a lot of forage. I want to explain how animals can help complete the system. I'm convinced God hates waste. He wants us to find creative ways to use the things we've been given. Consider food scraps from your kitchen. You could throw those on a compost pile. Nothing wrong with that. Over several months it'll break down and you'll use it to feed your garden. Alternatively, you could give those kitchen scraps to pigs, chickens, goats or other livestock and they'll turn those kitchen scraps into manure within a day. What takes the natural process a few months takes animals a single day. They are compost-making machines, but much faster. Animals complete the system.

Joel Salatin tells a story about a city in Europe where they decided to offer three free chickens to any resident who wanted them. Their goal was to reduce waste, and it worked! By the end of a year, hundreds of tons of waste that had been going into landfills was now being used to feed chickens!

While animals complete the system, I was grateful that Joel Salatin gave me permission to stop free ranging my chickens every day. In his Backyard Chickens talk at the Florida Homeschool Convention he said something like, "if you've got less than ten acres, why are you free ranging your chickens? Letting them poop all over your driveway and patio? Don't do that. It's not even good for all the bugs, spiders, and mites in your yard. Give them a chance to regenerate. Let your chickens out once a week for a few hours. That'll be enough." Whew! Thanks Joel. I needed permission from the grandfather of regenerative agriculture in the US to stop free ranging my hens 24/7 and not feel guilty about it. Sorry, hens, Joel said you guys stay in the coop!

I'm also growing plants to feed my pigs, some on purpose, and sometimes I feed them the wild plants that pop up in my food forest. Here are their favorites.

- Amaranth
- Avocado leaves
- Banana peels
- Banana leaves
- Brazilian Pepper leaves
- Cassava leaves
- Cassava roots
- Collards and other brassica leaves
- Cranberry Hibiscus
- Egyptian Spinach
- Firebush leaves
- Fishtail Palm leaves
- Longevity Spinach
- Malabar Spinach

- Mango leaves
- Marigolds
- Mulberry leaves
- Native muscadine grape vines
- October Rose (*hibiscus radiatus*)
- Pigeon Pea leaves
- Pigeon Pea green bean pods
- Red Mombin leaves (also called Hog Plum) and fruit

PARTING WORDS

You can do this. You're strong enough for this. You have what it takes. You were made for this. You can learn. You can grow. You can grow not only plants, but you can grow as a person. Your mind and heart will expand. You'll see the world differently. You'll begin to notice little things and you might start to wish things were different. Make changes where you can with what you have control over and give the rest to God. This is the path to peace.

Food forests make so much sense for all the reasons: our physical, mental, and spiritual well-being; for the good of the earth, our future, and our children. There are so many reasons to get back to connection with the land and what we were made for – sowing seeds and watching things grow. We do this with our plants, we do this with our words, and we do this with our lives. What kinds of seeds are you sowing? We reap what we sow.

Let's sow love.

Let's sow peace.

Let's sow kindness.

Let's sow patience.

Let's sow generosity.

The world has enough bitterness, division, fear, and apathy. Let's create beauty and abundance instead. Join the revolution.

Go grow!

Jen Reelitz grew up in West Palm Beach, Florida, surrounded by beautiful flora and fauna. She occasionally got to garden as a little girl when visiting her grandmother in upstate New York. It wasn't until later in life that her love of plants began to blossom. In addition, Jen spent a decade in non-profit fundraising, supporting the work of The Timothy Initiative around the world. Jen also serves as a founding board member of Recovery Church Movement and a third generation board member of Real Life Children's Ranch, in Okeechobee, Florida. Jen is passionate about food forest and wants to see more people and organizations embrace the model, creating beautiful landscapes that bear fruit.

Follow Jen on Instagram and Facebook
@jenreelitz

Keep up with her company
@foodforestdiy

Follow the book
@foodforestrevolution

So, you want to plant a food forest.

How would you like a guide to help you with tips on what to do eight weeks out, six weeks out, one week out, and on planting day?

To get your free food forest installation checklist sent to you, sign up for our email list at

www.foodforestdiy.com

9 798218 423223